W9-AOM-434

DISCARDED

(anatomy of a lie)

Other Books by Diane M. Komp, M.D.

As a matter of fact... Well, the truth of the matter is... To tell you the truth...

(anatomy of a lie)

Let's be perfectly honest here... And that's the whole truth... It was only a little white lie... Well, the truth of the matter is... Let's be perfectly honest here... It was only a little white lie... As a matter of fact... To tell you the truth... And that's the whole truth... As a matter of fact... Well, the truth of the matter is... To tell you the truth... Let's be perfectly honest here... And that's the whole truth... It was only a little white lie... Well, the truth of the matter is... Let's be perfectly honest here... It was only a little white lie... As a matter of fact... To tell you the truth... And that's the whole truth... As a matter of fact ... Well, the truth of the matter is... To tell you the truth... Let's be perfectly honest here... And that's the whole truth... It was only a little white lie... Well, the

the truth about lies and why good people tell them

DIANE M. KOMP, M.D.

ZondervanPublishingHouse
Grand Rapids, Michigan

A Division of HarperCollinsPublishers

Anatomy of a Lie
Copyright © 1998 by Diane M. Komp

Requests for information should be addressed to:

≝ ZondervanPublishingHouse
Grand Rapids, Michigan 49530

Library of Congress Cataloging-in-Publication Data

Komp, Diane M.
    Anatomy of a lie: the truth about lies and why good people tell them
  /Diane M. Komp
        p.   cm.
    Includes bibliographical references.
    ISBN: 0-310-21953-1 (alk. paper)
        1. Truthfulness and falseness—Religious aspects—Christianity.   I. Title.
    BV4627.F3K66   1998
    241'.673—dc21   98-26761
                                                                               CIP

This edition is printed on acid-free paper and meets the American National
Standards Institute Z39.48 standard.

Interior design by Sherri L. Hoffman

Printed in the United States of America

---

98 99 00 01 02 03 04 /❖ DC/ 10 9 8 7 6 5 4 3 2 1

To "Bad Dude Paul,"
a truly honest man

When we lie to ourselves, and believe our own lies, we become unable to recognize truth, either in ourselves or in anyone else, and we end up losing respect for ourselves and for others. When we have no respect for anyone, we can no longer love, and, in order to divert ourselves, having no love in us, we yield to our impulses, indulge in the lowest forms of pleasure, and behave in the end like an animal, in satisfying our vices. And it all comes from lying—lying to others and ourselves.

Fyodor Dostoyevsky, *Honesty*

(contents)

Part Six: Honest Hearts

(prologue: anatomy of a lie)

The truth will set you free.

John 8:32 (NIV)

The truth makes us free but first it makes us miserable.

Sandra Wilson, *Released From Shame*

On a rainy autumn Monday, too gray for hiking or other Alpine pleasures, I rummaged through the library of an old Austrian castle that had once served as a ski lodge for the European elite. Half-hidden between tall textbooks I found a slim memoir written by an American Civil War veteran. How H. Clay Trumbull's book came into Schloß Mittersill's collection is still a mystery to me. Embossed on the cover in gold-leaf script, lettered by an old-fashioned hand, was this title: *A Lie Never Justifiable.* No question mark followed the author's titular declaration.

As I read those four ornate, gilded words, a sliver of guilt shivered from some deep recess of my conscience, poking out a memory ahead of it. The incident happened the day I left for Europe.

Minutes before I was to leave for the airport, I dialed my favorite kennel to let them know that my Yorkie would be delighted to bunk with them while I was abroad. An unfamiliar voice answered the phone, a new kennel staffer.

"Are Babu's immunizations up-to-date?" she asked.

Nuts! I thought. Nuts, nuts, nuts!

Babu would have been the very model of canine medical compliance if my car hadn't broken down three days before. Just when the pup was due at the vet for his next round of baby shots, we were cooling our paws waiting for AAA to tow us to a repair shop. In the hectic days following that missed appointment, I never found another free moment to chauffeur Babu for his immunizations. In the competition between the dog's needs and other pressing chores, Babu lost out.

Five minutes before an airport taxi was due to arrive at my house, this new dog nanny had the nerve to upset my delicate pretravel balance. If I had answered her truthfully, the kennel would have denied my dog admission until he was immunized. So close to flight time there seemed nowhere else to turn, no other choice to make. "Yup," I lied, "Babu's up to date." I intended to deceive.

The cabdriver honked impatiently in the driveway, so I grabbed the dog and my suitcase and ran for the front door. At the kennel I noticed a bold new sign on the wall in very large print. IF YOUR DOG IS NOT IMMUNIZED, WE WILL DO IT AT YOUR EXPENSE. A second chance. Babu's reprieve. But I didn't take it.

At the kennel that day, my personal priorities seemed more important than the welfare of a loyal little Yorkie and the sensible requirements of a kennel. I could have told that young girl the truth. I just would not. How could I admit to her that minutes before on the telephone the venerable Dr. Komp had told her a bald-faced lie?

Sandra Wilson wisely observes that although the truth may ultimately set us free, first it makes us miserable.[1] At Schloß Mittersill, with that accusing book title burning in my hand, I felt wretched. There was no justification at all for the lie I had told. A reason, yes. But no excuse. The initial phone fudgery was for my convenience. My later silence at the kennel was for the sake of my pride. All of this was at Babu's expense. If there would be a penalty for my prevarication, it would be the dog, not I, who had to pay with his health. My lying could also affect other pets and kennel workers, but like most white liars, I didn't think of that at the time.

Perhaps there were other reasons why that time—and others—I haven't measured up to a standard that I've accepted for myself: to always be truthful. That's my standard, but it's not always my reality. Despite my best intentions (and other than the fact that none of us is perfect), why do I sometimes tell a lie? I wanted to know the answer to that question, even if it cost me my pride.

Thankfully, Babu outlived the experience, but it was something of a watershed event for me. Along with the questions raised by the book I discovered in the Austrian castle, my "harmless" lie prompted me to look deeply inward. Why, I asked, would I, a generally honest, Christian woman, *ever* tell a lie? During the rest of that trip through Europe and for the four months that followed, I kept a journal. That special diary is at the heart of this book.

In my journal I logged all the times that I failed to tell the truth or was even tempted to consider a lie. I paid attention not only to what I found in my heart but also to what was happening in the world around me. This project became the lens with which I viewed television, read newspapers, magazines, and books, and listened to my friends. How do we value and devalue truthfulness in our culture today? What I learned was startling.

My work as physician, writer, and speaker brought me face-to-face not only with the truth that I intend to tell but also with the potential for falsehood that shadows me wherever I go: in that Austrian castle and the American heartland, at a convention in Germany and my office at Yale, on the telephone with friends and at home in front of a roaring fireplace with Babu and a book competing for my lap. I noted as never before how the world cries out for truthfulness and how often we are betrayed. Worse yet, after we've been betrayed we throw up our hands and say, "What else could we have expected?" I saw firsthand how we demand the truth from others but in turn ourselves deceive. I wondered how often my own little lies contribute to the poisoning of our culture's well. My journal grew quite quickly.

As I write these truthful words about a lie, there is a part of me that secretly hopes you don't believe a word that I have said. A corner of my heart prefers that you overlook Babu's predicament and put your trust in my credentials instead: prominent doctor, trusted author. Recite my titles. (Don't listen to my words.)

If that glittering image of Dr. Diane Komp guides your judgment, you will interpret Babu's saga as a saintly example of dogged self-deprecation. But if you can't trust a doctor (or a saint) to always tell you the truth, if you can't trust yourself to always do the same, you bring us both—author and reader—to the reason I had to write this book and why you are reading it now.

In a world where headlines honk about perfidy in high places, there is something almost ludicrous about starting an entire book on lying with a little dog and a little lie. Surely you and I do not rank with the examples we read about in the press:

A police officer "testilies" to a grand jury.
A scientist fabricates crucial research data.
A naval cadet is dismissed from Annapolis for an honor
    code infraction.
An ambassador lies and buys his way into Arlington
    National Cemetery.
A president accused of lying under oath.

No wonder our world is in such a mess when we reap the effect of dishonesty trickling down from exalted positions into our ordinary lives. If the facts prove that our leaders lie, how can we expect our children be taught to value truthfulness? But please hear me out.

What if the cultural trend toward lying begins the other way
    around?
What if the trickle works from bottom up to top?
What if my own lies make a difference to the world?

What if, instead of shaking my finger at those in public life, I examined my own half-truths, puffery, and little white lies?

What if my "what ifs" are true?

I want to help myself—and you—live by the standards we've accepted for ourselves. So keep a journal yourself as you read, for it is your own illustrations—not mine, nor those of your spouse, your children, your parents, your boss, your coworkers, your roommates, your friends, your elected leaders—that can teach you the most about the anatomy of a lie. Be more than a reader. Be my companion for a lesson on the anatomy of our lies.

Systematically we will take a scalpel and pull back the layers of excuses, reasons, cover-ups, and socially sanctioned deceptions to learn why lying has become so epidemic. My hunch is that if we perform this dissection honestly, we will learn something that can change our lives. We might even learn something that can change the world.

Prologue Study Questions

1. How would you define lying?

2. Which of the following best describes your experience with lying?
    a. I never lie.
    b. I rarely lie.
    c. I sometimes lie.
    d. I lie fairly often.

3. Which of the following best describes how you feel when you lie?
    a. I accept my few lies as part of being human.
    b. I don't worry about it at all.
    c. I believe that lying is necessary in some cases.
    d. I feel guilty every time I lie.
    e. I need help to be a more truthful person.

4. What do you need to feel free from:
    a. Telling lies when you want to tell the truth?
    b. Feeling guilty about telling lies?
    c. Excessive criticism of those who struggle to tell the truth?

5. Start a journal to keep while you are reading this book. Record each time you are tempted to lie. Reflect on the times that you lie, or are tempted to, and ask yourself the question "why?"

PART 1

A Lie Never Justified?

Being forced to consider, in an emergency, the possible justification of the so-called "lie of necessity," I was brought to a settlement of that question in my own mind, and have since been led to an honest endeavor to bring others to a like settlement of it.

H. Clay Trumbull, *A Lie Never Justifiable*

CHAPTER 1

When Johnny Didn't Come Marching Home Again

So, within the prison cell we are waiting for the day
That shall come to open wide the iron door;
And the hollow eye grows bright,
And the poor heart almost gay,
As we think of seeing home and friends once more.

George Frederick Root,
"Tramp! Tramp! Tramp! The Boys Are Marching"

If you are honest men, let one of your brothers stay here in prison, while the rest of you go and take grain back for your starving households.

Genesis 42:19 (NIV)

Remember the book I found in the castle? *A Lie Never Justifiable* was too handsomely bound to be just a textbook. The elegant format hinted that a personal story rested within, rather than detached principles. What I found between its covers was both personal and instructive; it told the fascinating memoir of a Yankee Army chaplain who was held captive in a Confederate jail during the summer of 1863.

Today, we most often recall the American Civil War through romantic ballads like "Aura Lee," heroic anthems like "The Battle Hymn of the Republic," and nitty-gritty marching ditties like "Tramp! Tramp! Tramp! The Boys Are Marching" and "When Johnny Comes Marching Home Again." In a Brooklyn elementary school, my classmates sang those tunes as theme songs for our pre-pubescent gender war.

The fifth grade rallied round competing flags, dividing off as North and South. The boys were Rebs, we girls were Yanks. Across the playground, we shouted songs and slogans at each other. "The Union forever! Hurrah, girls, hurrah! Down with the traitor!"—that would be Richie Schmidt. "Up with star!"—hoisted by Betsy Mitchell, as I recall.

But the first modern war was neither a child's game nor a sentimental songfest. Charles Frazier calls this miserable era "a time that carved the heart down to a bitter nub."[1]

More than a century ago our nation was in tears as both armies claimed that truth was marching on its side. America, not Bosnia nor Rwanda, was rent in two. At the Battle of Gettysburg alone fifteen thousand lives were lost. Some say the wounds are still fresh and open today.

Captives sat in dank prisons dreaming of their final libera-tion. Better to die of typhus in freedom clutching your flag than to breathe your last surrounded by the foe. Prisoner H. Clay Trumbull must have had such dreams as well, including the day he found himself in the ethical emergency that inspired his book.

> Being forced to consider ... the possible justification of the so-called "lie of necessity," I was brought to a set-tlement of that question in my own mind, and have since been led to an honest endeavor to bring others to a like set-tlement of it.[2]

That is how this former Army chaplain opened his narrative when he sat down decades later to write about his fellow Federal captives' blueprint for escape.

When his friends first described their escape plan to him, Trumbull realized that the success of the entire scheme depended on telling a lie to their Confederate guard. His moral sense recoiled at the prospect of lying to an enemy solider. Trumbull was unable to go along with the plan.

Trumbull's fellow prisoners argued that war had suspended their obligation to tell the truth to those who had "forfeited their social rights." Trumbull, on the other hand, felt that irrespective of the circumstances, a lie was always necessarily a sin against God and was therefore never justifiable. *Never.*

Officers and gentlemen all, Trumbull and his sidekicks debated the dilemma. Would it not be more moral, one friend argued, to preserve that enemy soldier's life by telling him a lie than to sacrifice the man's life on their hasty path to freedom? Trumbull replied that he would not hesitate to kill that guard in an escape any more than he would have vacillated in battle if the same Confederate soldier had come up against him. It may not surprise you that Trumbull's comrades had some difficulty understanding this point of view.

> My friend then asked me on what principle I could jus-
> tify the taking of a man's life as an enemy, and yet not feel
> justified in telling him a lie in order to save his life and
> secure our liberty. How could it be claimed that it was more
> of a sin to tell a lie to a man . . . than to kill him?[3]

Trumbull was convinced that God and truth were on his side's side. At the time, however, he had to admit that he based his certitude about truthfulness more on his innate moral sense than on a single concrete principle that he could cite to his friends.

So this "Johnny" did not go marching home again with the others. At least not then. Trumbull chose to remain in jail until he could gain his release without dishonoring his deeply held beliefs about telling a lie.

What began in that Confederate prison under "circumstances that involved more than life" became a lifelong study for Trumbull when he returned to civilian life and the Congregational ministry. Thirty years later he put words to the principle he felt so instinctively and adhered to so passionately during that awful summer of 1863. Trumbull posited his ethical principle in what Scripture says about the character of God:

> The powers that be are ordained of God. . . . In the case then in question, we who were in prison as Federal officers were representatives of our government, and would be justified in taking the lives of enemies of our government who hindered us as God's agents in the doing of our duty to God and our government. On the other hand, God, who can justly take life, cannot lie.[4]

Few of our own moral choices allow us to study for a lifetime before we must respond. In a sense then, most of our ethical choices are "emergencies." Compared to the question before those imprisoned soldiers, the moral moments of my own life and the lies that I contemplate seem somewhat trivial. In my own lifetime, for example, I cannot think of a single time that I put either my own life or someone else's in jeopardy by telling the truth. But Trumbull's book intrigued me.

Whether or not my life's circumstances bring me to such unusual challenges, H. Clay Trumbull and I both base our ethical choices on guidelines laid down in Scripture, and like Trumbull I long for the character of God to be reflected in my life. I respect the depth of his scholarship, but like him I must search Scripture for myself to answer that question: Is a lie ever justified? So I turned to more ancient writings—the Hebrew Scriptures—to search for other ethical emergencies that might shed some light on the question.

Chapter One Study Questions

1. Do you think a lie is ever justified? Is it ever right to tell a lie? Explain.

2. Have you ever been in a situation where your own or someone else's life depended on whether or not you told the truth?

3. If you were given the choice of telling a lie to an enemy to spare his or her life or taking that life to spare telling a lie, which do you think you would choose?

4. If you were to come up against two competing moral imperatives, i.e. to be truthful versus to preserve a life, how would you choose what is the "right thing" for you to do?

5. Do you think that your enemies are entitled to hear the truth from you?

CHAPTER 2

The Hebrews' Midwives
and a Canaanite Whore

> The midwives answered Pharaoh, "Hebrew women
> are not like Egyptian women; they are vigorous
> and give birth before the midwives arrive."
>
> Exodus 1:19 (NIV)

> In the Bible, in the second chapter of Joshua,
> Rahab lies to the authorities in order to save the
> lives of the two Israelite spies. I don't recall read-
> ing about her trial.
>
> Oliver North, *Under Fire*

Do you think it is ever right to tell a lie? During the months I was journaling, I posed this question to my friends, colleagues, and even total strangers. I wanted to hear in their own words and with illustrations from their own lives what they thought about the so-called lie of necessity.

Some people I spoke with cited exceptions they deemed worthy of justification, but no one could give me an example from their personal experience to illustrate the point. Like Babu's dilemma and the examples from the headlines, their personal lies seemed to fall short of justification. But many people I spoke with pointed to two fascinating stories in the Old Testament where it appears that God approved of some outright lies. Did God really wink at the deception of the Hebrews' midwives and a Canaanite whore?

The haunting story in Exodus 1:15–21 of Shiprah* and Puah sets the stage for the birth of an important patriarch of ancient Israel. Without the midwives' civil disobedience to Pharaoh's mandate, Moses would never have survived.

With murder on his mind, Pharaoh ordered all midwives caring for slave mothers to report the birth of Hebrew male babies. Two midwives, Shiprah and Puah, sheltered these fragile lives by reporting to Pharaoh that the Hebrew mothers who gave birth to newborn males seemed to have extraordinarily rapid labor and delivery. Why, these women gave birth to boy babies so fast that the midwives never made it to a single male delivery on time! Never in their long careers as midwives had they ever seen anything like it!

The midwives deceived the deceiver, but were they justified in lying to Pharaoh? Some of us might think so, but not H. Clay Trumbull, who held that by biblical standards a lie is never justified: "God commended [the midwives'] fear of him, not their lying on behalf of his people, and that it was 'because the midwives feared God' not because they lied 'that he made them houses.'"[1]

If Trumbull had been a Hebrew dad, would he have allowed the midwife to lie on his son's behalf? Or would he have stuck by his principles and said, "God bless you, good woman, for your sentiment on behalf of my family, but God cannot honor a lie. Make your report as required by the authorities. I will depend on God to honor your truthfulness with perfect protection of my family"?

It is not at all clear from the Exodus text whether Shiprah and Puah were Jews themselves or Egyptian midwives assigned to the Hebrew mothers. Jewish tradition is split in this regard. The story is even more poignant if Shiprah and Puah's compassion was shown to aliens in their midst. Decades later one of those babies the midwives spared wrote these words that were given to him from God: "You shall love the alien as yourself, for you were aliens in the land of Egypt" (Leviticus 19:34 NRSV).

---

*Known as "Shifra" in Jewish translations of Exodus.

Pharaoh may be in his grave, but Shiprah and Puah's dilemma endures. By edicts of other tyrants, the same type of threat has revisited the Jewish people over the centuries. At several points in history, Gentiles have been drawn into a similar drama for the sake of God's ancient chosen people.

Some of those called to assist have stepped out of quiet private lives to deal in a very public manner with an extraordinary despot intent on shedding Jewish blood. Three Gentile magi from the East outwitted Herod's plot to eliminate the newborn King of the Jews, setting Herod on a murderous rampage. And in this century under the mania of Adolf Hitler there was another slaughter of innocents and opportunities for other "righteous ones"* to stand in the gap.

Read this account of life under the Nazis with the story of Shiprah and Puah in mind:

> "[F]or the clarification of scientific questions in the field of congenital malformations and mental retardation, the earliest possible registration" was required of all children under three years of age in whom . . . "serious hereditary diseases" were "suspected." . . . *Midwives were required to make these reports at the time of birth.* . . . Everyone proceeded as if these children were to receive the blessings of medical science, were to be healed rather than killed. The falsification [of the edict] was clearly intended to deceive—the children's families, the children themselves when old enough, and the general public. But it also served psychological needs of the killers in literally expressing the Nazi reversal of healing and killing.[2] [Italics mine]

This turnabout of healing and killing is exactly what Dietrich Bonhoeffer had in mind when he spoke of a reversal of truth and falsehood, the sort of duplicity that facilitates the slaughter

---

*"Righteous ones" is the term used by Jews for Gentiles who protected Jews during the Nazi Holocaust at the risk of their own lives.

of babies, whether by Pharaoh or Herod or Hitler. Bonhoeffer, a faithful German pastor whose life ended on a Nazi noose, had this to say about these types of moral choices:

> It is worse for a liar to tell the truth than for a lover of truth to lie. . . . There is a truth which is of Satan. Its essence is that under the semblance of truth it denies everything that is real. It lives upon hatred of the real world which is created and loved by God.[3]

My friend Ted vigorously debated this concept of the "lie of necessity" with his family. His brother, a pastor, held strongly to H. Clay Trumbull's position that a lie is never justifiable. Ted, on the other hand, took the position that not every false statement is a lie. Their fireside deliberations inevitably led to discussion of Adolf Hitler and his massacre of European Jews.

Ted's argument to his brother has a ring of Bonhoeffer in it: "Satan, as the 'father of liars,' would not have become a Dutch Uncle if they had said, 'Jews? Here?'" Unlike the faithful Hollanders who risked their lives to save Jews, Ted believes that Satan would have been glad to tell the SS the truth.

If you had been a midwife attending the birth of a handicapped child in Germany during the Third Reich, would you have been a Shiprah and Puah? Some German midwives completed truthful reports and later claimed they were only doing their duty, obeying the law.

While Scripture commends Shiprah and Puah for their Godfearing, Trumbull is correct that the Bible falls short of directly commending their methodology. Scripture informs us that the midwives' fear of God was greater than their fear of Pharaoh. Their fear to account to God for the lost lives of Hebrew children was greater than their fear to account to God for their lie to Pharaoh.

We do know that God was kind to these women, and their legacy lives on to this day. Their names are remembered with honor in the modern Israeli city of Tel Aviv where a large maternity hospital stands at the intersection of Shifra and Puah streets.

Trumbull understood the Canaanite prostitute Rahab's behavior (Joshua 2:1–22; 6:17–25) in the same way he processed the midwives' lie:

> [B]ecause of her trust [Rahab] put herself, with all her heathen habits in mind and conduct, at the disposal of the God of Israel, and she lied, as she had been accustomed to lie, to her own people, as a means of securing safety to her Hebrew visitors ... the Lord approved of her spirit in choosing his service. . . . She was not commended for either of those vices; but she was to be commended in that, with all her vices, she was yet ready to give herself just as she was.[4]

In essence, Trumbull does not exonerate Rahab for lying to her compatriots, but he does forgive her on the grounds that as an unbeliever, she didn't know any better. In doing so, Trumbull makes assumptions about aspects of Rahab's moral character that Scripture does not provide.

Augustine wrote about Rahab as well. He wished that Rahab could have had more faith. If she had been a courageous believer at the time, Augustine speculates, Rahab could have stood up to her fellow Canaanites, admitted that she knew where the spies were, but refused to reveal their location.

Somehow I don't think the methods of primitive torture were less refined in Joshua's day than our own. I have a hard time believing that such an answer would have saved the lives of the spies. I expect that under torture they would have extracted the spies' location from Rahab, and then killed her.

Herein lies my problem: I can only *imagine* how I would act if I were in a similar situation. I can recite the ethical principles, I can quote the Bible, I might even ask what is the fitting thing to do. But I cannot know for certain how I would have acted if I had stood in Rahab's place in that Jericho wall. Not even Trumbull could give principles for his refusal to lie back in that prison camp. He acted first, understood his spontaneous moral response later.

It seems sheer vanity for someone like me whose own life has never been threatened, or who has never been called upon to save a life with a lie, to imagine that I would come up with a more clever response than Rahab's own, one that would have upheld the scriptural proscription against lying *and* saved the lives of the spies.

Unlike my imagination, the genius of Scripture is that it presents reality. The books of Joshua, Hebrews, and James don't analyze Rahab or dissect her responses. They tell her whole story, then gracefully embrace her with unconditional love as a beloved and pivotal sister of faith. Everything we know about Rahab brings honor to this Canaanite whore who played an important part in God's plan for Israel. One Jewish legend goes as far as to say that Joshua made an honest woman out of Rahab by marrying her.

As Scripture charts the intersections of human lives with God's own story, it rarely paints a glamorous picture. There was room in that narrative for people like Shiprah and Puah and Rahab. There even is room there for you and me.

Chapter Two Study Questions

1. Do you think that the midwives' lie and/or Rahab's was justified? If so, why?

2. Do you think that the police are entitled to lie to a suspect in order to get the suspect to tell the truth?

3. Do you know any modern stories where people are in similar situations to the midwives and Rahab? What decisions did they make, and what was the outcome?

4. Rewrite the midwives' and Rahab's stories so that the spies' lives are spared *and* the truth is told. What are the consequences of changing the story in that way?

CHAPTER 3

The Saints of the Béjé

God himself made clothes for man.... Since the Fall there has been a need also for concealment and secrecy.

Dietrich Bonhoeffer, *Ethics*

You are my hiding place; you will protect me from trouble and surround me with songs of deliverance.

Psalm 32:7 (NIV)

Moral lives seem so much clearer when we can use a mortal enemy we recognize to put a face on evil. This chapter begins not with demons, however. It celebrates the lives of saints who struggled with truth telling. The book and movie *The Hiding Place* is just such a celebration recounting the remarkable heroism of Dutch Christians who hid Jews from the Nazis which took place in a quaint, narrow, little house on Barteljoristraat in Haarlem, Holland, that the Ten Boom family called "the Béjé."

You can hear things through the creaky floorboards in ancient houses like this one—three stories high, two rooms deep, and one room wide. A strange choice indeed for a hiding place. You can still enter the Béjé today through a watch shop in the Ten Boom Museum, just as when the family was living there half a century ago.[1] I bought a gold pocket watch in the shop this year and ascended to the family's living quarters by a steep, winding staircase.

Sitting in the Ten Boom's parlor, I listened to my guide fill in the family's history in loving detail. The characters in this amazing drama came alive through her recitation, assisted by photos and memorabilia covering every inch of wall. From the living room we moved to Corrie's bedchamber, the room that contained the famous hollow wall. Their Jewish houseguests had to race up steep, winding stairs in an emergency and enter this narrow space through an even smaller dresser drawer.

What did it feel like during the seemingly endless, adrenaline-pumped minutes that they stood there concealed in breathless silence until the Gestapo left? As I looked into the small, coffin-like space in which the Jews were hidden, I wondered how many of their guests might have experienced claustrophobia from the confinement. In a sweating moment of panic, I would have been tempted to break out of that wall or let loose with a scream. I felt my heart racing, my mouth drying as I peered inside the wall. A coffin is a coffin is a coffin.

It doesn't amaze me that Corrie ten Boom found the courage to risk her life to save Jews. What astounds me is that she was forty-five years old before she told her first lie.[2] Listen to Corrie herself narrate the story of that lie she told to a German army clerk:

> "Ten Boom, Casper, Ten Boom, Elizabeth, at the same address [as Corrie]. Do either of them own a radio?"
>
> I had known from childhood that the earth opened up and the heavens rained fire upon liars, but I met his gaze.
>
> "No."
>
> Only as I walked out of the building did I begin to tremble. Not because for the first time in my life I had told a conscious lie. But because it had been so dreadfully easy.
>
> But we had saved our radio.[3]

Reading her words today, I wonder what I would have done if I had had to stand in Corrie ten Boom's wooden shoes. When the Gestapo came, would I have lied to them about the hidden Jews? Or would I have told them the truth, then grabbed a gun and killed as many of the Gestapo as I could? Surely if any enemy has ever forfeited its "social rights" in the eyes of the rest of world it was the Nazis. There are contemporary theologians who might think that Corrie ten Boom went ethically too far. In his discussion of this type of ethical quandary, Walter C. Kaiser Jr. says that:

> Truth is always required in every other situation. . . . Thus when the Nazis of the Third Reich in Germany during World War II were asking if someone was hiding Jews, the correct procedure would have been to say as little as possible, all of which had to be true, while carefully hiding those Jews as best as one could.[4]

These questions are important because every day we are faced with numerous choices to lie or tell the truth, though with far less at stake. What guides our choice? What "special circumstances" allow us to lie?

I wanted to be certain that I understood Dr. Kaiser correctly. In the eyes of most of the world, Corrie ten Boom is a true saint of our century, someone whose example most of us would want to follow if we faced the same crises. I wrote to him, sharing what I had written in this chapter, and he was kind enough to reply:

> I read your treatment of Corrie ten Boom. Yes, I do believe you have understood me correctly in that I do believe that, in the case of the presence of two conflicting absolutes, we are not permitted to disobey either absolute that God has given, but that, in accordance with 1 Corinthians 10:13, God will in that situation also provide the way of escape. In Corrie's case, I believe she had a right to hide the Jews well and then to say nothing when asked whether Jews or others were present, but to invite the Gestapo to search on their own and to pray, therefore, that God would make them especially stupid so they would not be able to discover those that are hidden.

Kaiser does not stand alone here. There was one member of the Ten Boom family whose moral record stands in absolute agreement with him and Trumbull. Of all of the Ten Boom children, Nollie was the sister who from early childhood believed most firmly that a lie was never permissible. She reared her own children in the same belief. Two stories in *The Hiding Place* show us how remarkably consistent Nollie and her children were in this regard.

When they saw uniformed soldiers about to enter Nollie's house, two of her teenage sons hid in a concealed place below the dining room table while the women sat gathered at the table nonchalantly sipping tea. But it wasn't the women who interested the soldiers.

"Where are your brothers?" a soldier asked Nollie's daughter, Cocky.

She told him the truth: "Why, they're under the table." Cocky's answer sounded so absurd that one of the soldiers snarled that she shouldn't take them for fools. Then the soldiers left.[5]

Cocky's mother, Nollie, was very pleased. "God honors truth telling with perfect protection!" Nollie responded when she heard what her daughter had said to the soldiers. Corrie, on the other hand, spotted an inconsistent thread in her sister's rigid logic.

Had not Nollie herself participated in falsification of papers for Jews? In fact, Nollie had outfitted Jews in her own home to look like servants. Quoting Psalm 141:3, Nollie proof-texted her way through that situation: "Set a watch, O Lord, before my mouth. Keep the door of my lips."

But for Corrie it wasn't logical to speak the truth with your words but intend to deceive by your actions. Nollie, however, had not yet finished telling the Nazis the truth. The day that it happened, the rest of the family thought that Nollie had finally gone stark raving mad.

A young Jewess named Annaliese was in Nollie's living room one day when the Gestapo arrived. Pointing to the beautiful, blonde woman, they asked the mistress of the house, "Is this a Jew?" Annaliese's fair coloring offered room for a bold and cautious lie, but Nollie answered truthfully. She admitted that Annaliese was a Jew.

When Corrie heard what was happening at Nollie's house, she raced there just in time to see her single-minded sister leaving with men in brown suits. Behind them, the Gestapo pulled a pale and frightened looking Annaliese.

The Gestapo took Nollie to the local police station, but they planned to transport Annaliese to a Polish concentration camp and certain death. In a message that Nollie sent Corrie from jail, she defended her decision to tell the truth: "No ill will happen to Annaliese. God will not let them take her to Germany. He will not let her suffer because I obeyed him."

Six days after their arrest, Dutch resistance workers broke into the theater where the Gestapo were holding Annaliese. They released her and forty other captive Jews. Eventually, Nollie herself gained freedom and remained at liberty throughout the entire war.[6]

When the Gestapo arrived at the Béjé, Corrie followed a different ethical path than her sister had taken. When asked, "Where are you hiding the Jews?" Corrie lied. "I don't know what you're talking about," she answered. To the question, "Where are the Jews?" Corrie lied again. "There aren't any Jews here."[7]

Ultimately, the Gestapo arrested Corrie, her sister Betsie, and Papa Casper. A few days later the elderly Casper died in a regional prison. His daughters found comfort in remembering their father's words: "When the time comes that some of us will have to die, you will look into your heart and find the strength you need—just in time."[8]

The Ten Boom family did find that strength. Sister Betsie died in Ravensbruck, but Corrie survived that death camp to tell the whole world what happened in the Béjé.[9]

What did happen in the Béjé—at least, from God's point of view?

Nollie told the truth and was set free.

Corrie lied and was sent to a concentration camp.

Who is the real saint of the Béjé?

Does any of us even dare to judge?

Chapter Three Study Questions

1. Do you remember when you told your first lie? Think about why you can remember that incident.

2. Recall a time when telling the truth would have brought serious or unpleasant consequences into your life.
   a. Did you lie or tell the truth?
   b. What happened as a result of your choice?

3. Do you think God wanted Corrie to lie about the Jews she was hiding, or should she have trusted him like Nollie did to save the Jews another way?

4. If you had been in the Ten Boom's situation, whose choice would you likely have made—Corrie's or Nollie's?

5. If Corrie ten Boom were alive today, do you think you would trust her?

6. Read *The Hiding Place* and highlight what the different family members say about both lying and truthfulness.

CHAPTER 4

A Dining Room Brocade

A fine old family tradition is an heirloom as
precious as gold.
It is passed to each generation, embroidered as
it's retold.

Cathy Schrull, from *Never Alone*

No one can tame the tongue.

James 3:8 (NRSV)

Corrie ten Boom didn't tell a lie until she was forty-five. Quite possibly her sister Nollie never did. Unlike the Ten Boom family, most of us start evading truth very early.

By the time we were three years old, we had already figured out that we could use words to avoid punishment. Before we were five, we knew the impact that our false words had on our family and friends. We got what we wanted. And by the time we reached our eighth birthday, we knew the semantic difference between a lie and a mistake. Today we're no longer children, but we still tend to lie to avoid punishment and call it a mistake. We don't lie to save lives. We lie for a thousand little reasons.

Listen to the words of a clever little song that lovingly speaks of the tiny lies we dust on our family and friends each day as casually as we sprinkle confectioner's sugar on our breakfast waffles:

A fine old family tradition is an heirloom as precious as gold.
It is passed to each generation, embroidered as it's retold.[1]

I did some embroidery of my own in a restaurant the other day that I'm sure you will agree is charming. Loving, to be sure. And harmless. Or was it?

Sasha* is a recent college grad who had hoped by now to have found a high-paying engineering job. Instead, he's hoisting trays high at the Chowder Pot these days and is mighty, mighty eager to please.

"Did the Shrimp Florentine meet with your satisfaction, Madam?" he purrs to me. Ma-dam beams back her approval as she reaches for her VISA Gold.

My wallet falls open, revealing the photo of a sweet-faced baby, my little Crumb Bunny. Praying for a better tip, Sasha seizes the moment and coos, "Your daughter?" (Well, not unless Sarah and Elizabeth move over for another late-life miracle!)

"No," I explain. "My granddaughter."

Sasha bows respectfully from the waist, "You must be very proud."

I am proud. And in a way, I am Crumb Bunny's "grandmother"—albeit an honorary and not a biological one. At my hospital a few years back someone who didn't know that I was her doctor mistook me for one of her grandmas. In all the excitement that day about the bone marrow donation that was arriving from England to save the child's life, someone interpreted my loving enthusiasm as an emblem of relationship.

Is it a lie, really, for me to perpetuate this warm, cozy myth of kinship? More a half-truth than a lie, a proud piece of puffery. Perhaps even literary license. Certainly not as black as sin. Surely my tender words of appreciation for a fragile young life won't poison the entire world. What difference does it make after all, I tell myself, if a childless, middle-aged woman embroiders a harmless piece of dining room brocade?

---

*To respect privacy wherever appropriate I have changed some names and blended some stories throughout this book.

Rather than fretting over my little white lie, some contemporary ethicists would smile at me for puffing air into a shell of truth. There is a system of thought called "situational ethics" that links our choice of whether to lie or tell the truth to the context of our words, not to some moral rule about lying being right or wrong. "Not the 'good' or the 'right,'" said Joseph Fletcher, "but the 'fitting.'"[2] Unlike the author of *A Lie Never Justifiable,* who searched Scripture for the good and the right, Fletcher would never say never. For the situationalist, whatever feels right fits.

If, when I claimed the Crumb Bunny as my own, I meant well—if my motive to exaggerate was out of love for her—then so be it, says the situationalist, that I didn't tell the truth. What's the big deal anyway? If my motivation is loving, the situationalist would say that I have fulfilled the only necessary law—the law of love. But Michael Josephson, a former lawyer who subsequently turned ethicist, has a radically different opinion about lying.

Josephson is mightily concerned that these well-meant, so-called white lies we so glibly excuse can transform our entire society. Perhaps that's why Josephson has left the legal profession. Speaking of our individual lives and personal lies, Josephson insists that every untruth can undercut the very nature of truth and honesty itself. Every lie, Josephson declares, is a land mine.[3]

No matter how trivial a fib may seem to me at the time, no matter how loving my motivation might be, each lie I tell has the potential to hurt someone else. Even when I fib to a stranger whom I will never see again, there can be consequences that the stranger may later have to pay.

The strangest thing about half-truths is how easy it would be most times for us to simply tell the whole truth. That day at the Chowder Pot I convinced myself that Sasha had no real interest in hearing my answer to his question. He was only making chit-chat, I concluded, just warming up for a better tip. Does a brilliant young engineer cleverly disguised as a menial waiter really want to hear about me? Perhaps it is not Sasha but I who don't want to invest the time in the truth.

To avoid the initial awkwardness of truth, we sometimes tell half-truths or avoid the truth altogether by donning a prefabricated mask we've designed in our fantasy factory. But when we mask up, we miss the opportunity to watch truth bless those who would have heard it if we had only give truthfulness half a chance.

A while back I spoke to a group of women physicians who gathered to discuss the impact of their Christian faith on their personal and professional lives. One doctor came to that conference with her young baby. At the opening banquet, that tike made quite a hit. Weary after a long work week, we now had a special reason to relax and smile together.

Looking around the dining room I saw married women, single women, divorced women, mommies, mamma-wannabes, and not-quite-sure-about-motherhood gals, smiling women with smiling hearts, and smiling women with unseen broken hearts. Not all of us would know the delight to carry such a wonderful gift in our womb and deliver joy into life for others to share at such a moment.

"Children are important to all of us," I told that audience of professional women, "even for those of us who will never be biological moms." Then I told these woman doctors a story I had never told anyone else before—or since. Since I'm talking about honesty with you, I'll take the risk of telling you the story as well.

One of the things a women doctor learns early in her education is to put away her tears, even when the normal response would be to cry. You may not be a doctor or a woman, but perhaps you have retired your own tears as well. "It's not very professional." "Big boys don't cry." "I'm tired of crying." Name your own tear-stopper. But the most important day for us can be the day that we reclaim our canceled tears. For me, that date came soon after I came back to Christian faith at the age of forty.

I wanted to learn how to pray, so I asked a hospital chaplain to be my guide.

Toby caught me off guard when he encouraged me to ask God for a gift, the deepest desire of my heart. Right there on my knees I began to weep, but I still held back from being honest with God.

"No! No! I can't!" I insisted. Toby encouraged me to look into Jesus' eyes. "Tell Jesus about the deepest desire of your heart."

I resisted for the longest moments. Then, I told Jesus that I wanted a child.

There are those who might say that God never answered my prayer that day. I'm fifty-eight years old today and "barren," as King James English likes to put it. Perhaps God has never fulfilled my heart's desire in the way that I envisioned, but my prayer bore fruit at that conference when I told those women doctors the story of my recaptured tears. The next afternoon, other women wept and shared deeply from the gutters of their own hearts. We gave each other permission to cry.

A beautiful young mother mourned as she told the story of her infertility, then later the crib death of her lovely new adopted child. She and her husband were devastated by their double loss. More tears poured down her cheeks when she confessed her jealousy of that other mother whose baby stole the show at our opening dinner. Then, other women took off their smiley masks as well, and we all were healed as we listened to each other's true stories.

Back at the Chowder Pot, I should not have crossed over the line from fact to fantasy with Sasha. Oh, I'm not at all certain that he would have heard what I had to say, but I don't really know that for a fact. I should just honestly have said, "This is the child I always wished that I could have had." That is the truth. I love my little Crumb Bunny with all of my heart.

If I had told Sasha that truth instead of my charming little puffed-up lie, who knows what desires of his own heart might have had the opportunity to rise to the surface? His own long-ings might have been translated into healing words and recon-ciling tears.

Chapter Four Study Questions

1. What did you learn in your family about truthfulness?

2. Do you think half-truths, exaggeration, and little white lies should be considered as wrong and injurious as a deliberate act of major deception?

3. Give some examples of half-truths you have told or been told this week. How did they make you feel?

4. Think of an example of a piece of puffery you launched this week. How could you have told the same story and still achieved the desired outcome?

5. Think of an example of what someone else thought was a simple white lie that deeply hurt you. How did that affect your relationship?

6. For each of those examples of half-truths, exaggeration, or white lies, think about the other people involved and how you may need to set things straight with them.

7. Make two columns on a page in your journal. Each evening this week, reflect on your conversations of the day. For each communication where you intended to deceive the person you were talking to, make a checkmark in the lefthand col-umn. If your motivation was to protect the person you lied to, make the checkmark in the righthand column. Where do most of your marks fall?

PART 2

Truth Comes Home
to Roost

Politicians do it. Parents do it. We all do it. It's lying.

Ray Suarez, NPR's *Talk of the Nation*

CHAPTER 5

Doktor Di Meets
Bad Dude Paul

Even youths grow tired and weary, and young men stumble and fall.

Isaiah 40:30 (NIV)

Many and many a time I lied to my tutor, my masters, and my parents, and deceived them because I wanted to play games or watch some futile show or was impatient to imitate what I saw on the stage.

Augustine, *Confessions*

When it comes to truthfulness, some of our young people today court the darkness around them rather than letting light fall upon their words. Listen to this young courtier who calls himself the "Acid Warlock" on the World Wide Web:

> I truly believe that lying is one of the bases of society. Think about it, how many times do you lie in a day? Most likly [sic] more then [sic] once. It shapes and forms us. It twists what little morals we claim to have into a nice pretzal [sic]. Is there anyone left that has true morals? Were there ever any true morals to begin with? Why don't you ask your parent [sic] if they have ever lied, they will say yes and if they don't, they are lying again. And if you ask them about their parents, they would most likly [sic] say the same thing. Do I have true morals? Hell No. Today's world wouldn't work with morals.

I don't think most of our young people share the Acid War-lock's views. At least I hope they don't! But think about what the fellow says.

How many times in a day do you think a teenager lies? (Before you answer that question, though, think about how many times in a day you may lie!) There are published studies about the teen take on truth, such as one by Josh McDowell that found 66 percent of kids between ages eleven and eighteen admitted that they lied to a parent, teacher, or other adult.[1] Well, I think Josh is wrong, and here is how I know that it's just about as close to 100 percent as it can get.

About a month into keeping my journal, I started to look for companions who were willing to journal for just one week about their own experiences with falsehood. Very few adults to whom I issued this special invitation carried through. Typically, this is what I heard from them, "Well, maybe. But I can't do it this week...."

Could it be that "this week" they anticipated some situation in family life or at work where they knew that they would be tempted to lie? Yes, my friends admitted. They hoped to find a cleaner week later when they could let their virtue shine through their prose. Maybe in the spring.

Spring seems to be late this year.

Not everyone failed me, though. Amongst those who did commit to journaling with me for a week were seven teens who belong to the same church youth group. When I first proposed this project to these kids, I wasn't quite sure what to expect. These kids are very fond of me. They were unlikely to risk los-ing my friendship. But they took those risks, and told the truth about their lies.

In that week of journaling, each of my teen scribes recorded at least one lie to an adult. All but one had lied to a parent, and a little over half of them had lied to a teacher. But only one of them talked about lying to a peer.

Before you throw your hands up in despair, let me point out that these kids kept their commitment to journal and were very honest in what they wrote. Perhaps the most honest of them all is a sixteen-year-old who signed his journal "Bad Dude Paul."

His moniker was the first and only time Paulie has ever lied to me. The truth is, he isn't really all that bad, but the Dude thinks he can get the respect he deserves by taking on that name and persona. Strange, that he should adopt a phony identity, for not much in his worldview is worse than being a "poser."

From the get-go Paulie discovered that he was going to need all the help he could get to live through a week telling the truth about his lies. "I read my Bible study for the first time on time. Your letter got me thinking," he wrote. "I'm starting to worry about me. I feel messed up inside. It must be Doktor time for me."*

Interesting what kids lie about, though. Here are gleanings from the seven journals.

Clearly, loyalty is valued more highly than veracity:

- My dad saw me with some friends I know. I told him he was mistaken, but he was not. It was not worth the talking to about hanging around with the wrong kids.
- I lied for a friend about something so he wouldn't get in trouble with his dad. I took the blame so that his father wouldn't hit him or his mother.

Sometimes they lie to avoid the lectures they know will come if they were to tell the truth about their feelings:

- Was picked up by my dad [for visitation] and I told my mom I had a good time. God knows I hate his place.

And to avoid the lectures they undoubtedly would have received if they had been truthful about their school performance:

---

*"Bad Dude Paul" and his friends know me by the German spelling for "doctor" that I use for my E-mail address: DoktorDi@aol.com.

- Nothing big here. Just run of the mill. Told my parents my homework was done and I didn't even bring my books home.
- Went to my grandparents and told them I was doing good in school. I'm passing but not by much.
- I lied like a rug today. I failed two tests and told my folks that I passed.

One area that all the kids talked about was on the matter of lying to your friends about who you are—putting on airs, posing:

- I was a phony most of the day.
- I went to a rich neighborhood and pretended to live there.
- I was good today. I did not lie or be a phony at all.
- With me what you see is what you get, but I send false vibes because I talk so much.
- I really see no reason in my life to tell anything but the truth, and I do not like false impressions.

And at last, I've learned the mystery about going malling:

- Went to the mall with my best friend and played the role as I was her sister. That's neat. . . . People respect her more and she can get away with things.
- I went to the mall and pretended I was poor.
- Met a friend at the mall and was caught telling the organ store owner that I could teach him how to play. When he invited me to, I told him I had to meet someone.
- Met some friends at the mall and hung out. Didn't have any reason to lie.

Some of the kids—actually, most of them—talked with their parents about this weeklong adventure. I had messages from moms and dads sprinkled in their journals, but no true confessions from parents about their own struggles. More often, I heard how the parent had been victimized by someone else's lies:

- My dad said to tell you that his boss lied to him about having the day after Thanksgiving off. Now he has to work, and that makes me feel bad for my dad.

To teens, it's more important that other people tell you the truth than that you be truthful yourself:

- School was OK the whole week. No one lied to me that I know about.
- A kid told me that his family was at the park yesterday and that was a lie. His parents were home and so was their cars. It annoyed me more to be lied to then [sic] to lie. I used to like the boy.
- Talk about false impressions, we'll give him a chance to get with the script.
- So by walking out on the teacher like that, everyone knows she is a phony. I like that.

And how does it feel to lie?

- Yes I feel good about it.
- I have no problem with that at all. Would do it again.
- I hate to lie but lately I have to.

One year after their original weeklong journals, my teen friends were willing to write about lying once again. A lot has happened since they started to think about honesty. For some, there's been a trickle-up effect in their families as they talked honestly about their struggles to tell the truth.

Bad Dude Paul's Nana tells her grandson that he's got an awfully thick skull on his head. These days Paulie is listening to Nana. "I have a new thing I'm going to try," he tells me. "When I think I should say something I'm going to count to ten, if I still feel like I want to say it I will, but if in my counting my brain says don't, I won't."

Well, once his brain forgot to count, but his conscience bothered him so much that he called the person he lied to and set it right. This year his journal started with a warning to me that he wasn't going to have any lies to report.

But Paul also warns me that lying isn't the worst thing in the world that a dude can do. He feels far guiltier about his rudeness to a young girl who wanted to hang with the older crowd. More so than rectifying his lie, he's proud of himself for making that right.

My teen patients with cancer are more honest than the average adult patient. Okay, so they're blunt. Naked truthers (often) and their parents (sometimes) feel embarrassed. But teens make their doctors listen. We change our behavior. Isn't that what truth is supposed to do? Change us. Set us free.

I suspect if I had seven adults who had kept journals for me, the statistics would have been quite similar to the kids'. Would anyone have gotten through a week without honestly having to admit that they lied? Those of us who think we're responsible for teaching children how to tell the truth are starting from a serious position of disadvantage. But we do want to help kids, don't we?

It occurred to my journaling teen friends that they were not alone in their struggle to be truthful. They knew that their parents lied. They were pretty sure their teachers did as well. But they wondered about their beloved up-there-on-the-highest-pedestal pastor.

"Pastor Bob," one of the kids queried at an Ask-the-Pastor Night at church, "You kind of said that even pastors lie. Can you explain what you meant?" I'm not sure which took more guts— for the kid to ask the question in public or for the pastor to answer it before the entire congregation. This was Bob's response: "There was a time when I lost my focus. I walked around alone. I did not take God with me or let him join me. I looked around and said, 'Bob, you're great. Look what you have done.' Then

God showed me that this would have been done even if I had never been born, because God wanted this done. God told me, 'I chose you. Now stop the lying and get busy on my work.' So you see, I lied. Open and shut case."

With the help of a pastor who is willing to be open-and-shut-case honest, Paulie has made a lot of life-changing decisions in the last year. One decision has been to find a more truthful name. He's been trying out alternative monikers. This week he signed his letter to me: "From Paulie, The Main Dude (only the others haven't figured it out yet.")

But I have figured it out. It takes a lot of guts to be so truthful. That, Mr. Main Dude, is why I dedicated this book to you.

Chapter Five Study Questions

1. Do you think that adults are more or less truthful than the teens who kept these journals?

2. If your child or another young person asked you what was the worst lie you have told, how would you answer?

3. List ways you think parents can effectively teach their teens to be truthful with adults in authority positions.

CHAPTER 6

Mixed Signals

When we send our kids mixed signals, we get mixed-up kids.

Lee Strobel, *God's Outrageous Claims*

When parents come up to me and ask what they can do about their kids, I encourage them to be open and honest about everything.

Rebecca St. James,
quoted by Mike Yorkey in
"She Sings What I Want My Kids to Hear"

It's hard to be a parent today. It always has been. It always will be.

There are gut-wrenching days in my medical practice when I must tell a mom and dad a hard truth: their greatly loved child has a serious illness with a grim prognosis. If the child is old enough to understand, the next step is to talk to the parents about how to tell the child what is happening. Sometimes, the question is whether or not to tell at all.

This sort of truth-time isn't easy for a parent—or a doctor, but it becomes easier if our children have become accustomed to truthful adults. We prepare for these major moments when we tell the truth to children about situations that threaten us less. Such a dilemma was weighing heavily on my mind traveling by train through the Austrian Tyrol far away from my hospital and home.

Somewhere between Kufstein and the village of Wörg, I took out my computer and acquired a charming traveling companion forthwith. A ten-year-old Swiss lad seated across the aisle from me spotted my slick new Mac PowerBook. Daniel—that's his name, I learned—hoped that I had software games installed. I motioned grandly for Daniel to take the vacant seat just next to mine and fired up a round of Ultimate Solitaire.

After a few games of Klondike, I hinted gently to Daniel that I had work to do. Machts nichts. Daniel smiled and watched me type. But he did not move away. Ach, well. There aren't many days that something this sweet slips into my life unbidden.

Together Daniel and I turned my editorial travail into indoor sport. I let my new young friend click on the word processing palette to choose the colors for my revisions. New text—apple green. Strikethrough—cyanoblue. Daniel and I were content with our selections and keyboarded them into the computer's memory.

When the drink wagon came by, I asked him if he would like a soda. Daniel accepted my offer and drank from it briefly before excusing himself for a moment. He slipped into the compartment next to ours to check with his grandma. Was all right for him to accept my largesse? Oma approved. Daniel returned to my side and took another long large slurp.

"What did you tell your grandma?" I asked him in German, "that you found yourself another old woman?" Daniel giggled as he nodded yes.

Watching my manuscript appear on the computer screen, Daniel asked me when I had learned to write so well in English, a language he was just now starting in school. Swiss children can't tell the difference between an American accent on German and authentic Hanoverian Hochdeutsch. Vacillating between accepting undeserved flattery for my less-than-perfect German and 'fessing up, I told Daniel the truth. "English is my native tongue."

Outside our train breathtaking mountains were speeding on by. Picturing the well-groomed ski trails that soon would speckle Kitzbühler Horn, Daniel gazed longingly at the imposing peaks.

He confided that he prefers downhill skiing to the cross-country style. "You're a man, huh?" I teased. He nodded and grinned. Daniel began alpine skiing at the tender age of three.

"The Alps are so powerfully impressive," I marveled as we rounded the bend at St. Johann. "Are the mountains near your home as beautiful as these?"

"Beautiful, ja. And dangerous," he added, his mood some-what darkening. Like snowflakes children start to change the moment they are formed.

"Dangerous for the locals?" I wondered. "If you grow up in the mountains, you must know what to do to be safe."

"Lots of accidents," he repeated solemnly. "Lots."

Someone had told this child the truth. He knows that in seasons when the soft tinkle of a goat bell can trigger an avalanche, a child can perish. There are times a lad dare not yodel lest he loosen a breakaway slab of white death.

I remember my first visit to Daniel's country many years ago. For the entire cogged railway ride up to 11,333 feet through avalanche country, a Stephen King of a Swiss guide regaled us with chilling tales of man against the mountain and the mountain against the man. Listening to young Daniel I wondered if those stories might not be true after all, rather than alpine embellishment for tourists to supplement the sickening effects of thin mountain air at Jungfraujoch.

Apparently Daniel's family had not feared when they introduced him to the simple pleasures of mountain life that can not only enchant but also destroy. I would have had no fear to tell this child the truth about anything and everything. If Daniel had asked, I would have told him my whole life story. But he didn't ask.

From St. Johann to Zell-am-See I heard most of his life story, and a bit of his grandmother's as well (they were en route to her class reunion in Graz). Before bidding me farewell, Daniel thanked me for the Coke again, and moved out of my life as quietly as new falling snow.

After Daniel left, I snapped my laptop shut and looked out
the window. Lazy chocolate cows eyed the train, wondering if
they would see anything interesting today. Hadn't happened yet.
Shorn sheep hastened by. Crimson geraniums on fresh-painted
balconies. Don't their blossoms ever fade? Red tractors on green
pastures. Scattered husks of golden corn. And soaring peaks trad-
ing in their higher-than-the-treeline gray for a fresh gentle dusting of snowy white.

How poetic Daniel's mountain truth seemed in comparison
to my patient Pete's adventure. Other than his fear of needles,
Petey acted no more concerned the day I first met him than
Daniel did when he solemnly informed me that the beautiful
mountains can be dangerous as well. But there's nothing beautiful about cancer. Nothing beautiful at all.

"A merciful version of the truth" is what I call that gentle
dusting of words to tell a child of Petey's age that he is facing
death. No time for mere announcement or euphemism. Something lucid and gracious in between.

I asked Pete's mom what words she had chosen to tell her son
what was happening to him. Why did Petey think he was in an
oncologist's office that day? Nancy relaxed in her chair, confident
that she had revealed everything to her son. "We told him the truth,"
she said. "Pete knows that the lump on his scalp is 'lymphoma.'"

I saw no reaction in the deep silent pools of her son's brown
eyes as she spoke the dreadful word. "Lymphoma" may be cancer of the lymph glands to me, but it was not a term that held
power over Pete. I returned to Nancy's choice of words to frame
that disclosure. I asked her how she explained to Pete what this
thing called "lymphoma" was all about.

"Petey knows that there are bad cells in the lump, and that
these bad cells need to be treated with something called 'chemo,'
and that's why we are here."

It all seemed so cruel, to tell this child the truth. Every parent's worse nightmare. Worse than sitting outside the operating

room yourself and hearing the surgeon tell you the bad news for the very first time. How much do you tell your child? And, if at all, how do you tell your baby that he might die?

Pete looked too relaxed for someone who knew that something called "lymphoma" could kill him. I offered him a book written by a boy his age, *My Book for Kids with Cansur.*[1] He smiled when he saw the title, scrawled by a childish misspelling hand on the cover.

"This kid really is my age! Look at his handwriting!" Pete began to read slowly, phonetically. "Myyy buuuuk fooor kids wiith caaaaansuuuur. Can-sur. Cancer! I have cancer?" And then he melted into tears.

I returned to his mother's euphemism. "Petey, do you know the difference between 'bad cells' and 'bad boys'?" I asked him. "Or even bad behavior?" Petey looked at his lap and shook his head sadly.

Nancy grasped what I was working towards and recognized the problem with the phrase she had chosen to soften cancer. She had never intended to tell her son that he was a bad boy. She assured him that nothing he had done had caused the errant cell to make its could-be fatal error. The cells, not Pete, made the mistake. It was the cancer, not Pete, that was the mistake. Mom had not lied, but by not using the word *cancer,* she had postponed the truth. And for an apparently good reason.

Like most children, Pete had been watching and listening at home when no one thought he was paying attention. All those times at the dinner table when Mom and Dad talked about Uncle Rob who was dying from lung cancer, Pete heard what he learned was "bad behavior"—cigarette smoking—linked to cancer. "Bad cells happened to a bad boy"—that's the "truth" he thought he had heard about cancer. A mixed signal.

Nancy took Petey in her arms and assured him that his cancer had nothing to do with anything he had ever done. Even better, she reminded him that he had invited Jesus into his heart. All

his sins, anything bad he would ever do, had already been forgiven. This time she chose a metaphor that was good and useful,
refreshing and redeeming. Jesus in her baby's heart. Whatever
happened, Jesus would never leave her boy.

Once again the child felt safe. Petey looked relieved and
crossed his arms across his breast as if to hold Jesus there so
tightly that the Savior could never escape from his grasp. *Jesus
will never leave you.* Petey heard this signal loud and clear.
Thanks to his parents' preparation, he understood the whole truth.

Chapter Six Study Questions

1. Discuss examples from your own family life where your par-
    ents told you an important truth because:
    a. If you didn't know, you would have taken some action
        not in your own best interests.
    b. If your parents didn't tell you, you could have heard it
        from someone else other than your parents first.
    c. If your parents didn't tell you, there would be a tension
        in the family that affected your relationships.

2. If you are a parent, how have you dealt with telling your own
    children the truth?
    a. Unleash an avalanche of words
    b. Couch the truth in euphemisms
    c. Sanitize the truth for popular consumption
    d. Something lucid and gracious in between

3. How can a parent's lack of honesty with a child hurt the par-
    ent's ability to fulfill the obligation in Ephesians 6:4 to:
    a. Not exasperate their children?
    b. Train and instruct in the Lord? (cf. Ephesians 6:4)

CHAPTER 7

Holy Deadlock

Those who marry will face many troubles in this
life, and I want to spare you this.

1 Corinthians 7:28 (NIV)

People often lie most readily in marriage, exactly
because they fear losing the intimacy they have
achieved to that point. They know that nothing can
kill the fires of passion quicker than truth.

Stanley Hauerwas and William Willimon,
Where Resident Aliens Live

Listen to some blended stories.

"I'm so excited!" Sherri told me. Her husband, Art, is finally going to a Promise Keepers rally. That seemed very important to her. Sensing a shrill tone of desperation overlayering her electrified excitement, I wondered what Sherri expected Promise Keepers to do for her marriage.

"I hope they teach that lying buzzard how to tell the truth," she answered. And then she burst into tears.

I suspect that this little scene is exactly the type of situation that the apostle Paul—a bachelor—wished he could spare all believers. But most of us will opt for the joys of intimacy and not be spared such moments that blend desperation, excitement, and tears.

Like Luther's Ninety-five Theses nailed to Wittenburg's church door, the Seven Promises of a Promise Keeper are now taped to their kitchen fridge. "If he can't handle the Big Ten [Commandments]," says Sherri, "maybe he can handle just seven."

She's tried to straighten Art out before about the example he is setting for their children. At Sherri's insistence, their pastor has counseled him as well. Art, on the other hand, doesn't understand what the big deal is about anyway.

When Art catches their children in a lie, he takes a belt to them. Then, forgetting what he thought he was trying to teach his kids, he turns to his wife and lies about what he's been up to on the Internet. But Sherri's figured it out, all right. Yesterday she found an E-mail letter that Art forgot to delete from the computer memory. He says that this anonymous "Wanda9456" he met in a chat room is just a friend. He's never met this lady in person and he doesn't plan to, he says. That proves the innocence of his intentions, doesn't it?

This sort of rationalization drives Sherri stark raving wild. If he would lie about a cyber friendship, what else must he be lying about? Next stop in their holy deadlock is a football stadium and an ex-football coach who knows how to turn raw manpower into a weeping reconciling team. Promise Keepers is Art's last chance, Sherri says. The trust is gone. "How could he have lied to me?" she wails.

On a head level, Sherri thinks she is willing to forgive her husband for lying, but in her heart she wants to bring tears to his beady little eyes. "I want him to know what it feels like for me when he lies!" she hisses. Consumed by hypervigilance, Sherri asks me, "Does forgiveness mean I still have to live with the man?"

"People often lie most readily in marriage," say Stanley Hauerwas and William Willimon, "exactly because they fear losing the intimacy they have achieved to that point. They know that nothing can kill the fires of passion quicker than truth."[1] Let's hear a cheer for passion, folks, but let's have a robust round of applause for truthfulness in marriage as well. Who can afford the sort of intimacy that is founded on a lie?

Like Art, Dick hasn't been perfectly truthful with his wife in the past, but Margaret still wants to live with her man forever. "Maggie thinks I cross the line on half-truths," he confides to me quietly, thoughtfully. It didn't take Promise Keepers or any forces outside their marriage to make Dick listen to what his wife was saying. It simply took a heart that was able to listen.

Dick listened the night he was late coming home from work. It seemed so harmless to him at the time to say he was caught in traffic. But he also stopped off at the record store where that new Sinatra CD under his arm had come from. To him it seemed a trivial omission. To Margaret it wasn't trivial at all.

Dick is a conscientious Christian and highly moral person who admits that he doesn't have all the insight he needs when it comes to his own truthfulness. He felt convicted, not condemned, by Margaret's words.

Unlike Art, Dick is willing to hear the truth from his wife about his own untruthfulness. As hard as it may be sometimes, he listens lovingly to all that Maggie has to say. Oh, yes, Dick is more vigilant these days about his own behavior. He understands that how he handles his little half-truths has an impact on the most important relationship in his life. For Dick, the intimacy he gains through truthfulness with Maggie is far more important to him than his pride. When Margaret enters with love-light in her eyes and truth upon her lips, this man sees covenant spelled out as his rainbow in the sky. "Till death do us part" means doing the work it takes for their marriage to last.

Colleen used to be as irate as Sherri, but she never let it get that far. When her husband, Kevin, had a mid-life crisis, he broke her heart by emptying his into a different bed.

"Is Kevin still lying to you?" I wonder.

"No," she answers, "I said 'never again.'"

But neither did Colleen judge her husband as beyond forgiveness. "Kevin's not a bad person," she admits. "He just got goofed up for a bit."

Instead of withdrawing from Kevin emotionally, Colleen became a spouse-server.[2] "Am I better off with or without him?" she had asked herself when things were at their worst. When she looked at her marriage in perspective, she discovered far more reasons to work on her relationship with Kevin than to bail out. I listen to Colleen and wonder why one woman can forgive while another festers, so I ask Colleen about her mom and dad.

Raised in a strict Christian household where black was black and white was white, Colleen never lied to her parents because she knew the consequences. "I'd be killed!" she laughs. But she does laugh, and heartily at that. Colleen recalls her mother repeating countless times: "Oh, what a tangled web we weave, when first we practice to deceive."

Today Colleen doesn't lie, she tells me, and I believe what she says to be true. Neither does she remember hearing either one of her parents lie—ever. Thanks to her parents, truthfulness is the number one, most important virtue in Colleen's life. As important as it is, her parents also gave her room to forgive with head and heart and keep the husband who once lied to her about something as serious as another woman. No, she doesn't go to church anymore. She says she is burned out on her parents' "fifties-style fundamentalism," but she does have a personal belief and credits God with carrying her through the rough portion of her marriage.

Although Colleen has rejected her parents' brand of Christianity, she hasn't turned down what they taught in their home. Honest parents keep her an honest woman. Colleen believes that in the final judgment God will ask her to account for the things she has done here on this earth. And the things she has left undone as well, such as the times she's not forgiven. So not only does she not lie, she forgives.

For Sherri, truth was all-important but it was not the only virtue needed to support her marriage. As she withheld her trust and forgiveness, her marriage continued to crumble. For Dick, truth was hearable and doable because trust and commitment had made his marriage strong. For Colleen, her ability to forgive allowed her to maintain her own strong commitment to truthfulness without abandoning her marriage. None of these spouses would say that truth is unimportant, but in none of these marriages was truthfulness alone enough to survive.

There came a time in my own father's life when he wanted to talk to me about deception and forgiveness in our family. This conversation happened long after my mother's death, while Dad was showing some old color slides of past European trips.

Vacations just weren't the same for Dad after my mother was gone. The "happy wanderers," they had called themselves. That particular day Dad wanted me to know how much he loved my mother. Oddly, he expressed this love through a story about a time that my mother lied.

"We were in Italy," he said, "on the Costa Amalfitana." He let the Italian cadence wander lyrically from his mouth to my ear. "The scenery was breathtaking. Around every bend of the road was a scene worth painting. Constantly changing." True—I had just sat through two carousels, two hours worth of Saracen towers, deep gorges, dizzy bridges, and a sparkling, clear blue sea.

Dad described the marvelous dinner they shared that night in the village of Grotta di Smeraldo. He was chanting again, this time the complete menu of a meal he had eaten thirty years before. In the morning, he said, they checked out of a charming hotel and loaded their suitcases into a rental car. Then, the manager came out to the parking lot, mightily perturbed.

"Scusi, signor Komp-a, but the chambermaid she reports an-um irregularity. I'm-a sure there must-a be a logical explanation but the maid-a, she say-a that there's an ash-a tray missing from your-a room-a."

"I was livid!" raged my father. Knowing him, I believe it. "Your mother sat in the front seat of the car, not moving, looking all wide-eyed and innocent, as if she didn't know what the man was talking about. But I knew immediately where that ashtray had to be."

Of course he knew. Similar booty that my cigarette-smoking, ashtray-packing mama had amassed during other trips to Europe filled their living room at home. Mom had always assumed that a fine hotel intended for you to take the ashtray as an advertisement and a reminder to book there again.

Dad opened the car trunk and found the contraband in my mother's suitcase. Mortified, he returned the ashtray to the manager and sped away from that hotel as quickly as he could.

"The whole time, your mother sat there looking so innocent!" I believe that. I know that look. "I was speechless!" I believe that too. Speechless was my father's favorite style of communication.

I wondered how my parents' holy deadlock was finally broken and waited to see if I would hear. My father's mood changed, and a shy grin passed over his face as he finished his tale.

"Fortunately," he offered, as boldly as a modest elderly father can talk to his daughter about such things, "fortunately, that night our hotel room didn't have twin beds."

No, Sherri, lying isn't good, and humiliation does hurt. But forgiveness is as important as truthfulness. And yes, forgiveness does mean learning how to live with your mate.

Chapter Seven Study Questions

1. What is the relationship between truthfulness and trust?

2. What is the hardest lie you can imagine for which you might have to forgive someone?

3. As a child, how did you see your parents resolve their conflicts?

4. If you are married, how do you deal with half-truths, puffery, and those little white lies of your mate?

5. If you are looking forward to marrying, how do you plan to discuss your own attitude towards truthfulness and conflict resolution with your intended?

CHAPTER 8

Family Secrets

My wife, Shirley, says we have only two secrets left and if I tell those, I am dead meat.

Dr. James Dobson,
on "Focus on the Family"

So Delilah said to Samson, "Tell me the secret of your great strength and how you can be tied up and subdued."

Judges 16:6 (NIV)

In a tense moment in the movie *Exodus,* Ari ben Canaan (played by Paul Newman) and Kitty Fremont (Eva Marie Saint) lead orphaned European Jewish children to safety in the Promised Land. Saved from Hitler's Holocaust, their fragile lives are once again in danger. After the partitioning of Palestine, an Arab uprising threatens the kibbutz where the children live.

The time comes when they must all evacuate their new home in Dan Galfa for safer grounds. Since they must pass close to hostile Palestinian strongholds to escape, the party waits until cover of night to leave the kibbutz. Then the babies will be sleeping and the enemy cannot see.

Silently, the older children accept the burden of a little one in their backpacks. They will move on out into the night as a silent convoy. But first, one by one, Ari and Kitty tape shut the youngest children's mouths. If in their innocence these babes were to cry out, the whole party would be betrayed.

Every family has its private stories that are known by only a chosen few. Not everything that adults know do they tell to their children. Not everything that children learn at home should be told outside their families. There is a time to reveal and a time to conceal. But children don't always see it that way.

I was searching for a roll of scotch tape in my father's desk when I came across a handwritten genealogy of his side of the family. Bitten by the "roots" bug, I set off to dig as far as I could and find out more about who we are and were.

In Germany, Flanders, and England, my search for private ghosts turned up a pious lot of farmers, greengrocers, and country parsons. Highly respectable. Given the energy of my efforts, I suppose it was inevitable that I would someday open the wrong closet door and an ancient family skeleton would come rattling out.

It was more a taste for mystery than a bona fide search for truth, I confess, that kept me on the trail of this ancient clue that we were not all perfectly respectable. A snoop was born (but called it "research") when she smelled a juicy family secret.

I asked my father about the incident I had uncovered and was annoyed when it was clear that he had always known the story but had never intended to share it with anyone, including me.

"But why didn't you ever tell me?" I complained.

"What business is that of yours?" he retorted. "That's ancient history that should remain buried—where it was."

But I was like a pit bull, and I would not let the mystery go. I wanted to know that truth, assuming that truth always sets someone or something free. I enlisted the help of another relative and we set off together to find out as much as we could.

I regret that now. All this snooping turned up a secret far worse than the first, a mystery whose exposure adversely affected someone who is still living today.

Jim Dobson, who frequently illustrates important points on his radio program by personal stories, has this to say about discretion in family revelation: "My wife, Shirley, says we have only two secrets left and if I tell those, I am dead meat."

Dr. Dobson stands on good ground there, in not telling his listening audience everything that happens in his home. And he is not a less open person for having these boundaries between his private life and his "listening family." Even God operates his family on a need-to-know, limited info-access basis.

In the Garden of Gethsemane, Jesus informed his disciples about things yet to come: "But I have said these things to you so that when their hour comes you may remember that I told you about them. I did not say these things to you from the beginning, because I was with you" (John 16:4 NRSV).

Jesus did not keep this secret from his disciples forever. He held it until the proper time. Timing was vital. Even so, when he did disclose the truth about his coming death, sorrow filled his followers' hearts (John 16:6). You have to wonder how the disciples would have focused on their part in the ministry if they had been preoccupied with his death from the first time he called them away from their fishing nets.

This need-to-know basis even operates within the persons of the Trinity. After Jesus' baptism with the water and the Spirit, the Father still knew more than the Son about events that related to himself: "No one knows about that day or hour, not even the angels in heaven, nor the Son, but only the Father" (Matthew 24:36; Mark 13:32 NIV).

In contrast to those of us who are only human, Jesus did not delay telling his disciples the truth about his death because he could not bear the pain of their reaction to his revelation. Christ's decision, from his unique position of knowing more than they did, was entirely for the benefit of those he loved.

The example of the heavenly Father's relationship with his Son is a valuable guide to earthly parents who must carry out their own duties, but our families of earthly origin will always be fully mortal. Until we are no longer seeing through a glass dimly, we will not be able to fully consider the benefit of the child from whom the secret is withheld. Human parents will always be human. But we can try.

The decision to disclose or keep a family secret is not an easy issue, though. For every snoop like me who truly had no need to know, there's a hurting child consumed by a family's hidden shame.

I saw such a child in our hospital emergency room one night, crying out through her little body for help. It was one of many such ER trips for stomachaches. Usually they occurred in the nighttime. This time, a wise doctor started to ask other questions. This time, the answers to those questions hurt.

Nighttime is when Mindy has seen her mommy weep. She has seen as well what makes her mommy cry, when daddy starts to throw things at her mom. What the child had not been permitted to say with words, she had proclaimed through her pain. Until Mindy had a chance to talk about her fears, she would not heal. Held inside, the truth had made her miserable.

The family secret needed ventilation for healing words to be found and the whole family to be set free, but the closer the medical staff came to the source of Mindy's pain, the more agitated her mother became. At their local church, her father spun a tale to the elders worthy of a Peretti novel plot. The church applauded his efforts to keep the hospital from interfering with his rights as a parent. Eventually, her parents signed Mindy out and promised to follow up with their pediatrician. Instead, they changed doctors and galvanized their code of silence. Mindy's pain continues.

My friend Nancy also knows all about the perils of family secrecy. Her family invested a great deal of energy to perpetuate their clan mythology. Now she sees how this process has impacted her personal integrity.

Nancy grew up in an alcoholic household where family secrets wore the camouflage of official fabrication. She and her brother Tom eventually learned that their parents encouraged their children to lie to maintain the aura of respectability. But sister and brother still find themselves telling each other little white lies today when it would be just as easy to tell the honest truth.

"I told my brother, 'We don't have to do this anymore, to lie,'" Nancy lamented. "But we still do lie, and I don't understand why!"

Sandra Wilson has excellent advice for Nancy and Tom—and Mindy, when she grows up. Her words hold as well for any of us whose parents' secrets have had an adverse effect upon our lives: "Truth-based change comes from living new, truth-shaped choices."[1]

While the secrets may not belong to us, the choice to live free from the secret is clearly ours to make. If—and a big if—we are willing to forgive.

There is an art to searching for truth while loving those whose truth you are attempting to learn. Somewhere between the extremes of pathological lying and pathological fact-disclosure lies the safe passage through our family history. That safe passage contains within it the honoring of father and mother. "Honoring" does not demand that we share our parents' opinions or choose their methods to deal with our lives. But in our choice of how and to whom their secrets are revealed, we must treat our parents with respect.

I find myself struggling here, recognizing that there is no one solution for every family secret. It would be so much easier to say "never disclose" or "always disclose." But there is a starting question for me if I am that secret holder: *What is my true motivation for wanting to keep the secret?* Am I concerned with my own welfare or the welfare of the one from whom I'm withholding the truth? (Philippians 2:4). And a starting question as well for the one who needs the truth to set her free: *Even if I can never forget, am I still willing to do all that it takes to forgive?* The Bible suggests that if I forgive seven times a day, I still haven't forgiven enough (Luke 17:3–4).

A final footnote on my family's secrets. My grandparents spoke English with my father and uncles, and German with each other behind the children's backs. I had to learn German on my own and not at home since Dad couldn't speak or understand more than a few tourist phrases. Near the end of his life, after a stroke affected his brain, Dad heard me speaking German to a friend and seemed to understand. Surprised, I tried speaking German to him. Although he couldn't formulate sentences to respond, he certainly understood everything that I had said.

I wonder now what secrets my grandparents thought they were keeping to themselves behind their children's backs. I wonder as well if, in the end, there really is any such thing as a family secret at all. We would all do best to heed words of the ever-quotable Will Rogers: "Live so that you could sell the family parrot to the town gossip."

Chapter Eight Study Questions

1. Do you remember blabbing a family secret when you were a child? What were the consequences?

2. List ways that you think parents can teach young children to be truthful but also be discrete.

3. Write in your journal about your "family secrets."
   a. Give an example of a family secret that brought harm to others when it was revealed.
   b. Give an example of a family secret that brought healing when it was revealed.

CHAPTER 9

Eloping Home

I prepare for my death then, first of all by claiming for myself the truth of who I am. I am someone who was alive in God's heart before I was
born, and will be alive in God's heart after I die.

Henri Nouwen, On Death and Aging

My power is made perfect in weakness.

2 Corinthians 12:9 (NIV)

Alarm bells rang wildly as her electronic bracelet alerted the
staff that Nelly was "eloping" from the nursing home. This
elderly woman was out the front door and almost to the road
before the chaplain arrived on the scene.

"She said she was going home," Chaplain Kathy told me, "so
I gently escorted her back to her room by telling her that I would
take her home."

Ministering in a long-term care facility with more than ninety
Alzheimer's patients, Chaplain Kathy often finds herself telling
less than the whole truth. I tried to give Kathy margin for her
interchange with this elderly woman by asking this question:
"Isn't it true that the nursing home is her home?"

Kathy didn't jump at my offer to credit her statement as truthful enough. She admitted that she had intended to deceive. At that
moment in that old woman's mind, the nursing home wasn't her
home at all. Kathy knew what Nelly meant because she had been
there before, up close and in her own family's home.

Convinced that her husband would commit suicide if he was told the truth, Kathy's mom spun a tale that the mental changes were related to some surgery Dad had gone through ten years before. The doctor joined in the collusion, and this became the official family myth. "My mom is mentally competent," says Kathy. "I respected her decision."

Respect, yes. But is it justified to lie to someone just because they are legally incompetent?

Her mother's choice is rooted in history. Lying to patients with a poor prognosis was routine and considered "humane" in the early 1960s when I started medical school. It was considered the loving thing to do in those days, especially for children and elderly folks.

Historical, yes. But is it right? "Old patients," says Erikson, "seem to be mourning not only for time forfeited and space depleted but also . . . for autonomy weakened."[1]

Only when we put ourselves in the place of the vulnerable old can we fathom their need to know about their own lives and distinguish their necessities from our personal need to control. And the desire to assume control over another human heart is the basis of most human lies.

Is it your turn yet to be an adult child caring for an elderly parent? My turn came a few years back. It's scary and confusing. Far more appealing to take off the mantle of daughter and replace it with a long white doctor's coat. It's inviting to become the parent and reduce them to children, and it's tempting to trade in honoring our parents in favor of controlling them.

Once my father's health began to fail, he held onto his independence with the tenacity of a Green Beret. It was so hard to fly from Connecticut to Ohio each time! Weary from my own over-busy life, I had scarce energy on the weekend to take on anyone else's. After ten hours' work each day at the hospital and telephone-interrupted sleep every night, I had to race to the airport on Friday afternoon with just barely enough time to catch my flight.

Once when my flight was canceled, I was stuck in Newark, New Jersey, of all places. Miserable airport. I hate it! When they finally located a functional plane and the flight was ready for boarding, I spotted a friend. David Bryant, a praying man. From Newark to Cleveland we caught up on things that had happened since we last had met.

David was going to Ohio to lead a "Concert of Prayer," and the organizing committee for the event was meeting him at the Cleveland Hopkins Airport gate. After brief introductions, he asked his friends to take a few minutes to pray for my family. Other deboarding passengers gaped at this laying-on-of-hands in a public airport. Whoever heard of people praying in an airport, for heaven's sake?

That moment of grace carried me through a very difficult weekend. It helped me lovingly tell my Dad a very difficult piece of truth. He was no longer safe at home.

The time finally came when, like Chaplain Kathy's woman at the curb, my father was ready to run. For Dad, the alternative was the same. There was no place to run to except back to a nursing home room.

"I want to get out of here!" my father roared. He was impatiently wheeling himself around at the front door when I arrived. He had made it to eighty-six years of age, but was no longer competent.

"Competent" is a legal term, even if doctors get to make the call. But competence isn't a judgment over an old man's every thought or an excuse to dictate every movement of his life. I didn't want to control my dad. I just wanted to tell him the truth.

"This is home, Dad," I said. "The house isn't there anymore." I'm glad he didn't get to see his house the way that I had on the way in from the airport. Vacant, except for a ladder sitting in the middle of the living room. The home he had tenderly cared for had turned into a handyman's special.

My daddy wept for a moment, and then he took my hand. "I'm so glad you're here, Di," he said. No matter how else his brain now failed him, he never failed to tell his twin daughters apart. He kissed my hand, moistening it with his tears. As we went back to his room, he spoke about the other nursing homes he had been in. He'd seen firsthand what three other facilities were like before this one. He might not be legally competent, but he wasn't stupid.

"As places like this go, this place isn't really bad. The staff are nice. Very kind."

When the time came to leave again for the airport, I said my good-byes. "Thank you for coming," my daddy said.

Home is where grace and truth can live together, and find rest.

Near the end, as my father was dying of cancer, I had to make some difficult decisions about his care. He was not only incompetent now, but unconscious. I had only his advance directives in front of me, fifty-five years of being his daughter, and my sister by my side. To my discouragement as a physician, the hospital staff were no help at all. Converting his directives into responsive medical orders became a major chore. But I was determined to honor my father with a faithful translation.

The strangest thought entered my mind at that moment, sitting there by his bed in the ICU. It was as if I had to tell the truth about his wishes, because somehow my father would know what was happening here on his behalf.

The statistics say that one of these days, I'll be a Nelly, or just like my dad. That's a hard truth to hear, not easy for someone who adores solitude to think about living in chaos. My entire adult life I've only had a dog at home to talk back to me, and I must say I've liked it that way. On my last sabbatical year in Germany, I decided to see what it's like for someone fairly set in her ways to live with other people in community. A dry run for the future nursing home, I called it.

In a quaint half-timbered house in Marburg, not unlike the Ten Booms' "Béjé," I lived with ten other people, some of whom I had never met before. To mimic nursing home reality, I made one rule for myself that year: if the going gets tough, this toughy can't get going. "You have to work it out," I told myself.

It only took a week before I was fantasizing about a private apartment and checking out classified ads. But I stayed, and I'm glad.

Besides the wonderful friends with whom I lived, there was one important reason why I was able to endure. In that house, we told each other the truth about what drove us crazy. And we listened to others when they complained.

When I am old and inKOMPetent, please tell me the truth. And listen to me as well before I elope back Home.

Chapter Nine Study Questions

1. Discuss examples from your own family life or other experience when someone had to tell an elderly person a difficult truth. What made it possible for the truth-teller to be truthful?

2. Discuss examples from your own family life or other experience when someone lied to an elderly person. Why did that happen?

3. How do you want your family, friends, and caregivers to deal with the truth when you are:
   a. Elderly, competent but stubborn?
   b. Incompetent?

4. How will you communicate your wishes to your family, friends, and caregivers?

PART 3

It's an Ethical Jungle Out There

Although "white lie integrity" may be normative, it is not spiritually healthy.... It subtly expands and leads us ... into a kind of uncritical acceptance of all kinds of dishonesty.

J. Keith Miller, "White Lie Christianity:
The Beginning of Spiritual Leukemia"

CHAPTER 10

The Fudge Nudge

The trouble with the rat race is that even if you win, you're still a rat.

Lily Tomlin

The race is not to the swift or the battle to the strong, nor does food come to the wise or wealth to the brilliant or favor to the learned.

Ecclesiastes 9:11 (NIV)

Since 1951, the United States Naval Academy has had this honor code: "Do not lie, cheat or steal." Recently, the Academy learned that students no longer come to that campus with the moral upbringing that enables them to work under that simple behavioral paradigm. Superintendent Admiral Lynch, whose own career was cut short when he failed to take rapid action against a large-scale cheating scandal, finds that this basic honor code is a drastic "culture shift" for today's cadets.[1]

In previous generations, midshipmen came from homes that taught them to always tell the truth. Today, the service academies can no longer expect that their cadets learned to be truthful at home. According to *The Barna Report*, 72 percent of Americans aged eighteen to twenty-five—college and graduate school age—believe that there is no such thing as "absolute truth."[2] Gene Veith argues that those who do not believe in truth are more likely to tell a lie.[3]

Nothing is more bizarre than the case of one expelled midshipman who appealed (unsuccessfully) to the Supreme Court,

claiming that the Academy's honor code "failed to meet the min-
imum standards of fundamental fairness."[4] Apparently he did not
think it was fair to expect students to tell the truth.

It would be easy to blame a generation for their inability to
discern truth from falsehood, but these young people did not
develop their ethics in a vacuum. My friend Greg is juggling a full-
time job with graduate school this semester. In one of his courses,
Greg missed the deadline for his final paper, but his professor
offered him an excuse that would allow him to pass the course.

"I was preparing to turn in my grades," the prof told Greg, "and
I noticed that I didn't have your paper. I was thinking that with the
UPS strike, perhaps we had a case of something lost in the mail."

Greg realized that he had a perfect setup. His prof had
already passed him the fudge nudge, offering permission for the
lie that surely would follow his opening generosity. As much as
Greg wanted to pass the course, he fought the temptation and
told the man the honest truth. He might not pass the course, he
thought, but he did feel a surge of energy and power. "The truth
did set me free," Greg later observed. But it bothered him deeply
that a professor was promoting dishonesty in his students.

In retrospect, what worries Greg most is what might have
happened to him if he had accepted his professor's invitation to
lie. He would have been further entrapped in a chain of follow-
up lies. "What then?" Greg wonders. "'My computer crashed
and I'm trying to retrieve the files,' and on and on and on."

In another course he's taking, Greg saw how deeply seated is
the academic fuzziness about truth these days. In a seminar on con-
sumer behavior, the professor made a list of factors on the black-
board that motivate prospective buyers to purchase a particular
product. At the top of her list was: "Their own personal truth."

Didn't the professor mean personal "belief" rather than truth?
Greg wondered. No, she insisted. She had carefully chosen her
words. Personal truth was what she meant, even if that included
two mutually exclusive "truths."

Another classmate agreed with Greg and used a historical example to argue against the professor's premise. Not too many centuries ago people believed that the world was flat. Was the world in fact flat just because some people believed that was "true"?

Greg and his classmate are correct. Not even sincerely believing something makes it "true," any more than Linus can make the Great Pumpkin real by faithfully waiting for him on Halloween every year. But in a market-driven ethic where the customer is always right if she's got her wallet out, it sounds friendlier to upgrade beliefs to the level of truths.

Culture-watcher Gene Edward Veith observes that the goal of trendy scholarship in these "postmodern times"* is:

> ... "no longer truth but performativity"—no longer what kind of research will lead to the discovery of verifiable facts, but what kind of research will work best, where "working best" means producing more research along the same lines ... so that the question asked by teacher, student, and government must no longer be "Is it true?" but "What use is it?" and "How much is it worth?"[5]

Some ethicists teaching at our universities today tell students that not only is truth relative but that the obligation to tell the truth is relative to the situation. This sort of relativism leads students to believe that either:

- lying is neither right nor wrong (since there are no laws); or that
- lying is only generally wrong (in a world where there are no universal laws).

---

*"Modernism," that grew out of the Enlightenment, challenged a single worldview based on religious truth and favored a single worldview whose truth was provable by the scientific method. "Postmodernism" now challenges that truth is ever knowable, and challenges science's pre-eminence in favor of many worldviews, even if those differing worldviews are logically mutually exclusive.

The notion of "creating truth" may be novel, but its consequences are as ancient as the Garden of Eden. A *USA Today* article calls this brand of creativity the "Higher Education Sellout":

> Colleges are founded on truth. Their mission for centuries has been to seek it out and dispense it. Unfortunately, in the billion-dollar business that getting into college has become, truth often takes a back seat. . . . If truth and honesty are declining values in society, our kids are learning it early— when they knock on the college door, or someone knocks for them.[6]

This ethical relativism has had a profound effect on student behavior. Some college professors seem to have thrown in the towel on truth.

"You could almost grade excuses," mourns Southern Illinois University history professor Dale Bengston. "High marks [would] go for creative excuses." Bengston wonders why, when a delinquent student finds it necessary to kill off a grandparent in a tale to spare a grade, that grandmas are more likely to take a fabricated nosedive than grandpas.[7] Oh dear granny! What ever happened to *veritas* in college education, where the support garnered from grandparents was in the values they taught rather than the excuses their advanced age provided their young ones?

Lux et Veritas. "Light and truth." That has been the motto at Yale University where I teach ever since it was founded as a Congregational seminary. For the earliest students, a behavioral code explained how the faculty expected "light and truth" to be translated into daily communal behavior.

> All students shall be slow to speak and avoid . . . lying, needless asseverations, foolish garrulings, chidings, strifes, railings, gesting, uncomely noise, spreading ill rumor, divulging secrets, and all manner of troublesome and offensive behavior.[8]

Yale's founders didn't feel the need in those days to ask what truth or truthfulness were. They were certain their students had learned the obligation to be truthful at home and in their churches. Today some of our Yale faculty question whether some tenets in the founders' statement on student behavior might rob our students of their constitutional right to free speech. But other colleges that never before had honor codes for their students have instituted codes as an attempt to curb the alarming disrespect for truthfulness they see on campus.

What happens when today's caught-between-the-culture-and-a-hard-place students apply their "personal truths" to their academic work? The headlines of the *Chicago Tribune* told of one scandal that shook the scientific world: DISCLOSURES OF FRAUD ROCK GENE PROJECT.[9]

When the investigation into the work of a graduate student was complete, he was accused of numerous examples of fabrication and misrepresentation. These fudged results were an integral part of not only his doctoral thesis but as many as six scientific articles coauthored by his highly respected mentor, Dr. Francis Collins.

Although Collins himself was not accused of complicity, journalists and colleagues wondered why the deception had not come to his attention earlier. In an open letter, Collins acknowledged that "many will wonder whether I as the research mentor was paying sufficient attention to this individual, if such deliberate and systematic assaults on scientific truth were occurring."

Of four ethics seminars at Yale School of Medicine this year, one seminar title summarized the expectation that we will be truthful about our work and mean the same thing about truth-telling: "Data Handling: There Can Be No Fudge." By offering these seminars, the medical school realizes that they cannot depend on what we as faculty members and students learned from the universities that educated us.

All four seminars emphasized honesty, integrity, and a common standard in how we do our work as scientists. There was no hint that truthfulness in research is a relative concept. As the seminar title stated, there can be no fudge. And yet, such relativity is being widely taught in liberal arts and the humanities.

In an educational institution like a medical school we cannot afford anything but a healthy respect for truthfulness. We must mean the same thing when we're talking about telling the truth. I'm sure that even academic relativists hope that the doctors who take care of them have a narrow view of truthfulness.

Chapter Ten Study Questions

1. Can you think of any situation where you think that it is not fitting for you to tell the truth?

2. How do you think parents can best equip their children to honor truthfulness as a way of life in their academic careers?

3. Review your own academic career. Journal about the difficulties you faced then in being totally honest and why you now think you had those difficulties.

4. What did you learn about truth telling from your teachers in high school, college, and graduate school?

5. Do you think it is imposing personal beliefs on students to tell them that honesty is an absolute standard?

6. Give an example from your experience of a lie you told when you were a student that had a wider impact than you imagined at the time.

CHAPTER 11

Business As Unusual

Customers expect salesladies to praise the mer-
chandise, that's only natural. But I don't expect you
should outright lie. God would consider that sinful.
But then what would God think about the [other]
lies I tell?

Bette Greene, *Summer of My German Soldier*

But now be so kind as to look at me. Would I lie
to your face?

Job 6:28 (NIV)

When my friend Larry leaves home for the small retail business that he built up from scratch by the sweat of his brow,
he would like to take his Christian ethics with him. In practice,
though, he has come to believe that integrity and honesty do not
work at work. Sadly, Larry's concluded that the Nazis knew what
they were talking about when they said that the big lie sells.

If you don't buy into lying for the sake of being the fit sur-
vivor, Larry says, your competition surely will. So sometimes he
lies, but mostly he exaggerates. At the end of the work day, he
locks the door of his shop and hopes that he is leaving duplicity
behind. "Hopes," I say, but his family would like to offer him a
second opinion on his level of success.

Oh, that it was that easy to divide yourself in two. Grey-
tinged business ethics follow us directly to the hearth. "Business
as usual" means putting organizational goals above personal

moral standards. Even above our families. The least acceptable of all our lies are the ones that we bring home.

Like Sherri's husband, Art, we tell our children that lying is bad, while lies are part of the daily fabric of our work lives. "We justify the inconsistency by saying that all lies are not equal," observes management consultant Peta Penson.[1] It's just that some lies are more agreeable to us than others.

"Business as usual" is the message Larry's son Jonathan has heard from good old Dad. Sonny has come to agree with Pop that not all lies are equally wrong.

Jonathan is in college now and plans to take over the family business when Larry retires. Actually, Jonathan thinks about truthfulness a lot these days, most often when he's in love. That seems to be quite often.

"I could never date Melanie again if she ever lied to me, even once," Jonathan says resolutely about his current flame. This girl he describes as a "keeper." Maybe. He's never caught her in a lie yet, but if Melanie ever lied to him about something as trivial as what movie she and her roommate went to see last night, Jonathan's trust in her would instantly evaporate. Poof! Jonathan prides himself that he has never lied to any of his sweethearts and expects the same courtesy from them. "How can you have an intimate relationship with somebody who lies?" he asks rhetorically, but then he hasn't asked his dad. Perhaps he should.

Would Jonathan go along with H. Clay Trumbull all the way to never? No way! He is Daddy's little boy and always has been, even when he's lied to Daddy. Jonathan would call it "socially acceptable" to lie to your parents. Or school teachers. Or your boss. Not only acceptable, but even necessary. Just like his dad, Jonathan has bought into a bottom-line way of life.

From *Mayberry RFD* to the LAPD, even the police are lying on the job these days when the truth doesn't seem to fit the situation. Although the Supreme Court has endorsed deceptive tactics with suspects, not all of our police officers agree.[2] While some struggle to find a truthful way to get the same information from a suspect, others lie freely. Some even cite Rahab as an example that in the war on crime, all is fair if you're the one wearing the white hat.

One Christian policeman I spoke with has been thinking deeply about the problem that he calls "dirty hands." Although Walter has never been one to condone situational ethics, he can conceive of situations where he could condone a public servant who lied on the job. In retrospect, though, he's uncomfortable with the times that he has coaxed a suspect into a backseat of his police car by telling him, "You're not under arrest right now." Although he's done that to protect himself from a potentially violent person, he doesn't like to do that. "Usually I don't," Walter says, "though I know it is done routinely by others."

Attorney Gerald Uehlman illustrated the magnitude of public distrust in lying cops by comparing testilying Detective Mark Fuhrman to an exemplary biblical liar. "Fuhrman," he said, "is possibly the greatest liar since Ananias." The public doesn't trust a police officer who might lie to them any more than a child trusts parents who function with a double standard. "Do as I say, not as I do" has never worked for anyone.

Few of us caught in the moment of a lie—an "ethical emergency"—have the objectivity to put our lie in perspective. To Ananias, his lie was trivial. To God, Ananias's lie was lethal. Thus, New York City's police Inspector Belfiore has said that, "The only way [for the police] to win . . . respect and credibility back is with the truth. What we're trying to teach officers is that the truth is what is most important."[3]

A detective I spoke with works in the North Carolina town where *Mayberry RFD*'s "Aunt Bea" (Frances Baviar) retired from her acting career. In Siler City, where people are proud to be compared to Mayberry, some members of the police force watch old reruns of *The Andy Griffith Show* as a kind of "continuing education in moral law enforcement." In one particular show, Sheriff Andy exaggerated the value of an old cannon he was fixing to sell. The impact of this easy duplicity came back to haunt him when he saw his son, Opie, imitating his lie. In the end, Andy was honest about the value of the cannon because he saw the danger to his family if he practiced a double standard.

It's not just Larry and Jonathan, Andy and Opie, Ananias and Fuhrman who are in trouble, but all of us who work in an ethical jungle. My own journal had embarrassing examples from work. It's not the big lies that trip me up on the job, but those little, not-so-white ones:

- I put that report in the mail yesterday.
- I don't remember hearing a message like that on my voice mail.
- I was too busy with a patient to get to that meeting.

But there are clear and clean ways to demonstrate occupational integrity. My friend Randy models business-as-unusual to his clients and to his family.

Randy made an expensive error about the specifications for a motor on one job a while back. His first instinct was to blame the manufacturer rather than admit to his customer that he hadn't done his homework right. As Randy thought about it, he realized that the money wasn't the impetus to lie as much as an unwillingness to admit error. "It hurt to admit that I wasn't the wunderkind of environmental systems after all."

So Randy made the costly ethical choice to tell the truth. His business hasn't gone belly up yet, but he has succeeded to take his integrity to work with him and home again at night.

It's not that it's easier for Randy than it is for Larry and Jonathan. Randy has been down that other path of the big lie before, marinated in beer up to his eyeballs. His face gets dark when he thinks about that time of his life. When Randy speaks of the spiritual conversion that followed those dark days, he describes a total transformation of his life—an integration of mind, body, and spirit, at work and home.

Randy likes the feeling of living with a clear conscience. He will never estimate success based on his bank balance again. His family likes his honesty as well. Living by a single standard, he can afford to bring the office home with him and take home back to work with him again.

Chapter Eleven Study Questions

1. Is there any discussion about ethics in your organization or profession?

2. Do you find yourself in conflict with the ethical ethos on your job? How do you deal with those conflicts?

3. Do you consider yourself more or less ethical than your colleagues?

4. Can you think of any examples in your family life where ethics at work had an impact on home life?
    a. Was that impact positive or negative?
    b. Can you now think of a better way that situation could have been handled?

5. Should we hold some people to a higher standard than others when it comes to truthfulness? If so, which professions?

CHAPTER 12

Duplicitous Divines

All the way along the centuries, while the strongest defenders of the law of truthfulness have been found among clergymen, more has been written in favor of the lie of necessity by clergymen than by men of any other class or profession.

H. Clay Trumbull, *A Lie Never Justifiable*

The idols speak deceit, diviners see visions that lie; they tell dreams that are false, they give comfort in vain. Therefore the people wander like sheep oppressed for lack of a shepherd.

Zechariah 10:2 (NIV)

Come join me as we witness Hester Prynne's disgrace. You can bring the children with you to the scaffold today because the hanging will only be a figurative one. Not too messy. 'Twill be good for their little souls to see the village biddies string up Miss Hester with their much-exercised, well-muscled tongues.

Hester was just released from the local dungeon today. She still must wear a scarlet letter *A* embroidered on her bosom as an example to the rest of Puritan New England of what sinners can expect when pious Christians catch them *in flagrante*.

The local gossips marvel at their own mercy. Why, the court could have passed the biblical sentence of death upon the hussy! But the adulteress has yet to name the deplorable sinner who partnered her offense. Once more the community attempts to force his name from her lips.

"Exhort her to confess the truth!" a senior divine entreats the young pastor of this local flock.

At the foot of the scaffold meet the Reverend Arthur Dimmesdale, a most accomplished weasel-wordsmith. In response to the congregation's demand, Dimmesdale comes forward from the crowd to question Hester, his head bent low as if in silent prayer. Listen with me to his words:

> Thou hearest what this good man says, and seest the accountability under which I labor. If thou feelest it to be for thy soul's peace . . . I charge thee to speak out the name of thy fellow-sinner and fellow-sufferer! . . . Believe me, Hester, though he were to step down from a high place, and stand there beside thee, on thy pedestal of shame, yet better were it so, than to hide a guilty heart through life. What can thy silence do for him, except it tempt him—yea, compel him, as it were—to add hypocrisy to sin? . . . Take heed how thou deniest to him—who, perchance hath not the courage to grasp it for himself—the bitter, but wholesome, cup that is now presented to thy lips![1]

Permit me to interpret for any modern reader who may have difficulty translating this deceitful speech out of Dimmesdalese:

> Hester, sweetheart, this guy is my boss—kind of like a Puritan bishop. You know I'd really like to just jump up there on the scaffold with you. My conscience has been killing me all the time you were in jail having my baby. I don't have the guts to confess the deed myself, but on the other hand, if you wanted to confess for me, that might actually save me from a sin worse than adultery and lying, that of becoming a hypocrite. God, how I hate hypocrites! You could save me, Hester. You know, I really envy you. You're one gutsy lady, and I wish I was standing up there with you. But it's all up to you, honey. My future and fate are in your hands. Do the right thing.

Although Reverend Dimmesdale stayed strictly within the bounds of literal truthfulness, he conveyed no truth at all with his speech. He told the sort of slippery truth that Dietrich Bonhoeffer calls satanic. "Under the semblance of truth it denies everything that is real."[2]

But would these Puritans ever have forgiven their pastor if they had understood the hidden truth in his words? Dimmesdale didn't want to take that chance. He took his secret with him to his early grave.

H. Clay Trumbull notes that, "All the way along the centuries, while the strongest defenders of the law of truthfulness have been found among clergymen, more has been written in favor of the lie of necessity by clergymen than by men of any other class or profession."[3] Could it be that holding up a standard from the pulpit and living with the same humanity as your congregation is a heavier burden than we pew potatoes care to admit?

Ask the Malcolm Wright family what the consequences are when a pastor lies to himself, lies to his family, and lies to his congregation.

Malcolm Wright Jr. stands convicted of the first-degree murders of an African-American couple who were walking down a well-lit street in their own neighborhood, minding their own business. Other than hatred, there seemed to be no other basis for the act. At this young racist skinhead's sentencing, his father pleaded with the jury to spare his life.

A second-generation drug addict and felon himself, Malcolm Wright Sr. experienced a jailhouse conversion. Wright so impressed some of the Christian friends who ministered to him in prison that after his release from jail, they invited him to shepherd a church. Without formal pastoral education, he led this independent church from a mere handful worshipping in an old building to a thriving five-hundred-member congregation. The church appeared to flourish until the pastor began to live a lie.

Wright seduced a married church musician into an adulterous

affair that destroyed her marriage as well as his, divided the church, and separated the father from his son. The pastor divorced his wife, married the other woman, returned to drugs and scams and prison, where he once again repented.

There were clues in Malcolm Wright Sr.'s story that should have been red flags to his jailhouse supporters. A rousing personal testimony is no substitute for seasoned maturity. An independent church is a poor choice for someone who needs accountability as much as a new convert who once was a successful con man. As sincere as Wright Sr.'s testimony rang, at times there was a lingering hint of a con wringing out one more abuse excuse.

Throughout his trial for murder, the son showed no emotion. He gave the jury and other observers no reason to empathize with his plight. Only through the repentant father's testimony did any sense come into Malcolm Wright Jr.'s sad life story.

One piece of evidence supported the father's candid confession of his sins visiting his next generation. The court read a letter into evidence that the defendant had written in his early teens. This document revealed the impact of the father's duplicitous life on the development of a fragile boy.

Don't non-Christians thrive on these sordid tales and use them to indict all pastors and all of Christianity? Frankly, I was reluctant to give as much room to this topic as I have. But the outside criticism is not without merit. Duplicity from those with authority over our spiritual lives carries dire consequences for us all, especially for those who turn their backs on faith because a pastor has lied to them.

The data in *The Day America Told the Truth* illustrate that in an era when we have lost confidence in the public school system, we trust grade school teachers more than we trust pastors.*

---

*Out of a possible 4.0 highest score, Patterson and Kim gave the following grades: firefighter 3.07, pharmacist 2.91, grade school teacher 2.88, Catholic priest 2.81, Jewish rabbi 2.73, Protestant minister 2.64, medical doctor 2.64, police officer 2.47.

In his ministry to churches, David Bryant has seen firsthand why it is important to insist that there be no little or great land mines in the body of Christ. "Oh, boy, I'd better not get going here!" Well, I think I will get David going on this subject the next time I see him. This is not a topic that will be without illustrative examples any time soon.

"Your work on truth telling is so much needed," Dave Bryant told me. He believes that one of the great sins of the church is duplicity. "I see it everywhere, especially among spiritual leaders."

But the rest of us must take part of the blame ourselves. When we ask pastors to stand on a pedestal as part of their job description and be more honest with us than we expect to be ourselves, we turn them into hardened heroes. Asking to be deceived, we are partners in duplicity.

Chapter Twelve Study Questions

1. Should a pastor be held to a higher standard than the lay leadership or members of a church?

2. How would you feel if you caught your pastor in a lie?

3. What can church members and lay leaders do to help a pastor be accountable?

4. List the most important authority figures or role models in your life.
   a. How would you feel if they lied to you or someone else who depends on them?
   b. How can you adjust your expectations of them to not hold them to a higher standard than you ask of yourself?

CHAPTER 13

A Lawyer with
His Torts on Fire

The Burlington Liar's Club offers membership to
all except lawyers and politicians. "They're professional liars," said the club vice-president.
"We're just amateurs."

Quoted by Carmine DeSena in
Lies: The Whole Truth

[Jesus] taught as one who had authority, and not
as their teachers of the law.

Matthew 7:29 (NIV)

After he saw the film *Liar Liar,* my friend Al moaned, "Terrible!" This retired lawyer's blood pressure rose as he watched
his least-favorite, rubber-mouthed actor (Jim Carrey) prance
across the movie screen demonstrating why the Burlington Liar's
Club rejects lawyers for membership. "They're professional
liars," said the Liar's Club vice president. "We're just amateurs."[1]

Although Al is an honest man himself, the movie made him
squirm. His early retirement from legal practice was in part
prompted by what he sees as the deterioration of his chosen profession.

James Patterson and Peter Kim find not only the legal profession, but many service professions today in a serious state of
ethical decay. To research their book *The Day America Told the*

Truth, Patterson and Kim turned to the public for answers. They wanted to hear people like you and me tell who we find to lack credibility. Perhaps predictably, they found that 40 percent of us think that a lawyer has lied to us. That statistic fits our expectations. But look at who else we group together on the bottom rungs of our trust-ladder:

- TV evangelists
- senators and congressional representatives
- prostitutes
- organized crime bosses
- drug dealers

Thirty-two percent of the people surveyed said that a member of the clergy has lied to them. That is only 8 percent fewer than those who said that they had met up with a lying lawyer.[2] Thus, *Liar Liar* could be the story of any of us who falls back on something other than the truth to get through an ordinary working day.

As the film opens, we see a fitting metaphor for the effect that lies can have. A drop of water falls into a pool, creating ever widening ripples.

Meet five-year-old Max Reede, child victim of divorce. In his kindergarten class, the kiddies are learning about W-O-R-K. The teacher asks the children what their parents do for a living.

"My mom's a teacher," says little Max proudly. "And Dad?" the teacher wonders about the parent he doesn't even mention. "He's a liar."

The shocked teacher attempts to correct the darling little boy. "Oh, I'm sure you don't mean a *liar!*"

Although nouns seem to have failed him, Max knows how to paint a word picture. His dad wears a suit and goes to court and talks to a judge.

"Oh, I see!" exclaims his teacher, visibly relieved. "You mean a 'lawyer.'"

Max shrugs. "Liar" or "lawyer"—aren't they both the same thing?

When we meet his dad, we learn quickly why young Max is so confused. Follow Fletcher Reede (played by Jim Carrey) through a day, and any honest person would squirm. Squirm, because Fletcher's day isn't that different from our own.

Fletcher tells a beggar that he has no change he could give him.

Fletcher tells a receptionist that her extreme new hairdo "accentuates" her features.

Fletcher asks his secretary to lie for him on the phone.

Haven't we all been in these same situations ourselves? Listen to some embarrassing parallel notes from my journal that make me squirm:

- I told a neighbor collecting door to door for the American Heart Association that I had already "given at the office."
- I told a boring colleague that he gave a very "provocative" grand rounds.
- I begged my secretary to tell an HMO case manager that I wasn't in.

As much as I'd like to deny it, there's a touch of Fletcher Reede in me.

In the Reede family saga, we quickly learn that the lawyer/liar ethic spills over onto Fletcher's home life as well. This makes living tough for a little guy who can't depend upon his daddy's word. Fletcher may fool the people at work with his practiced smiles, but his five-year-old human polygraph machine doesn't fall for a phony word his daddy says.

Max had hoped that his dad would keep his promise to come to his birthday party, but Fletcher lies his way out of that one as well. Feeling rejected, Max finally blows out the candles on his cake, but not before he wishes that his father would not tell a lie for one entire day. This being Hollywood, even that kind of magic is possible.

On total-truth day, Fletcher revisits each of the situations in which he had lied the day before. With all the discretion of a lobotomized three-year-old, he tells the beggar that he does have change in his pocket, but he sure won't give it to him. Fletcher not only refuses to give him a handout, but he takes the opportunity to lecture the bum on his personal role in the decay of Western society.

When the receptionist with the outrageous hairdo asks Fletcher what he thinks of her outlandish new dress, he tells her, "Whatever. It takes the focus off your head." And in the courtroom, he's a lawyer with his torts on fire. Unable to dissociate his body language from his provocatively truthful words, he's a wreck who waxes biblical. "I'm getting what I deserve. I'm reaping what I sow." Watching Fletcher Reede turn ploughshares into swords, one would have to ask if the truth is always warranted.

In an attempt to hold onto his sanity (if not his impulses), Fletcher tries to explain to Max the way he sees the world. "Sometimes grown-ups need to lie," he tells his son. "Nobody can survive in the adult world if they had to stick to the truth. Everybody lies. Even your mother lies sometimes."

Ah, Saint Mama! How clever to invoke the name of Max's one reliable parent. Note that Fletcher did not say, "Even Mother Teresa lies." But then, Mother T. never had to live with lie-a-minute Fletcher Reede. "You're the only one who makes me feel bad," Max tells his dad.

Near the end of the film, Fletcher meets up with the same beggar. This time, he cheerfully gives him money, but he also shares an important lesson he has learned during the twenty-four hours he had to tell the whole truth and nothing but. There is more to life than money, Fletcher offers. Pleased with his new-found life, Fletcher tells himself, "This truth stuff is pretty cool."

In the end, Fletcher Reede changes not because of the rightness of the rules, but out of the goodness of love for his son. After the mandatory truth-telling period has expired, he keeps the "mother-of-all-promises" out of his own free will.

Al did find one redeeming virtue in the film. "After the laughter dies down, some of us may do some serious reflection about the ease with which lies are a part of the currency of communication." But *Liar Liar* is as much about truthfulness as it is about lying. The film points out why truthfulness sometimes gets a bum rap.

Fletcher Reede should have been held accountable to keep his promises to his son, but the man had no obligation to blabber every uncensored thought that flooded through his tortured brain. If we based our personal moral choices only on the lesson of this film, we might give some serious thought to whether truthfulness is anything more than moral gas. Instead, we need to discern between big-mouthed fact tattling and authentic God's-honest truthfulness.

Chapter Thirteen Study Questions

1. Look back at the three situations in which Fletcher Reede told a lie. What is your own score form 0–5 with lying in similar situations as he did?

2. Why do you think that the legal profession has such a negative reputation with the public?

3. Take the situations from the film in which Fletcher lied and see if you find any similar examples in your journal thus far.

PART 4

The Truth Always Warranted?

There is nothing as powerful as truth—and often nothing so strange.

Daniel Webster

CHAPTER 14

Busybodies and
Other Fact Tattlers

A gossip reveals secrets; therefore do not associate with a babbler.

Proverbs 20:19 (NRSV)

The abuse of truth ought to be as much punished
as the introduction of falsehood.

Blaise Pascal, *Pensées*

I began this book with the conviction that I should always tell the truth, but also with the knowledge that I didn't always meet that standard. After reading the memoir of a deeply committed Christian who could more easily kill a man than lie to him, I found myself questioning whether there are lies that can be justified. Here's a companion question to that, the dark side of unrelenting truthfulness: Is the truth always warranted?

I doubt that any viewer of *Liar Liar* was totally comfortable with Maxwell Reede's total-truth day. If you asked the question, "What is wrong in this truth picture?" you're with me. The film could have distinguished between truth telling and fact tattling. But it didn't. Let me illustrate what I find to be the difference by sharing a story I heard on the radio program "Focus on the Family."

Dr. Dobson's guest that day told the story of a child I'll call Sally who spends a good portion of her day snitching on her little brother. In counseling the family, she advised Sally's mother to issue a prescribed number of tickets per day that her daughter could use to rat on her brother. After Sally used up her tickets, her mother would not allow her to tattle on him any more that day.

Listening to his guest's advice, I could hear Dr. Dobson chuckle. "If I were that little brother," he reflected, "I would make her use up her tickets in the morning, and then I'd have the whole afternoon free."

Now, Dr. Dobson is someone passionately concerned with truthfulness. In this story, however, he recognized the difference between Sally's activities and the noble notion of telling the truth. The distinction begins with the difference between *the truth* and *a fact*.

Sister Sally was working with a *fact*.

Facts are pieces of information that are verifiable, and, in that sense, facts are true. Our legal system works with facts, and juries look at facts when they seek the whole truth and nothing but. Scientists deal with facts when they use the scientific method to examine the world. In turn, those of us whose lives are impacted by jury verdicts and scientific research all depend on reliable witnesses to tell those facts in a truthful manner.

If, for example, you were asked to consent to a risky form of cancer treatment, wouldn't you want—even need—to assume that the doctors whose research formed the basis for that treatment had been totally honest in working with the facts to produce their result? But the measurements themselves, what the doctors observed, are not "the truth." They are facts that need to be interpreted by a reliable witness. The truth itself is a far weightier matter.

Sally's mother was responsible to deal with the *truth*.

Within its substance, the truth carries not only the substance of facts but also the consequences and appropriateness of their disclosure. There should be a legitimate reason why a particular fact bearer becomes the truth teller.

The truth is so sacred a concept that a serious accountability rests upon its deliverer. Those responsibilities distinguish a truth teller from a busybody—an ordinary gossip:

- A truth teller should have an appropriate reason to assume the mantle of revelator.
- A truth teller should adequately investigate as many facts involved as necessary before speaking.
- A truth teller should examine any ulterior personal motives to make the facts involved known publicly.
- A truth teller should have empathy for anyone whose life may be affected by the revelation.
- A truth teller should consider the timing of disclosure.

In tattling on her brother, sister Sally was far more interested in securing her own position in the family than serving the interests of truth. Clearly, the child's motive to "tell the truth" was in question. Furthermore, Mom was unlikely to appoint this little girl as enforcer of the family morality. Sally's mother required no additional data to understand the little brother's nature, and if Mom did she surely would not have assigned this daughter to obtain that information.

Significantly, Sally expressed no empathy for her brother, nor understood his point of view. When she self-righteously brought his behavior to the family light, her focus was on her potential gains, not the moral improvement of her brother. And finally, her timing was inappropriate. Sally should have waited until her mother asked her for any such information. So should most of us.

In church life, one of the saddest examples I see of fact tattling is the misappropriation of spiritual authority to "correct" those "caught in a sin" (Galatians 6:1). Paul offered this admonition to a local congregation where there was an established loving relationship between individuals. Instead, as in the case of Hawthorne's Hester Prynne in *The Scarlet Letter*, some take what they've heard about others without following Paul's companion instruction to be gentle and watch, lest you yourself also may be tempted. Only when we examine ourselves to discern

whether we, as outlined above, are authentic truth tellers, do we
carry each other's burdens, and thereby fulfill the law of Christ
(Galatians 6:2).

My friend Harry is relearning the distinction between "a fact"
and "the truth" through his own beloved grandchildren. Harry
writes:

> My five-year-old grandson is already grappling with
> "what is a lie?" He feels that ignoring any ugly sound or
> unpleasant odor is a form of falsehood. His mom is trying
> to teach him that good manners are sometimes in conflict
> with pure candor. I can imagine the contributions he will
> eventually make to our ongoing family discussions!

We are not born understanding the needs and feelings of the
other people in our lives, not even the most important others. As
"little strangers" to the rest of the family, we arrive on the human
scene as new neighbors with a sense of our own needs alone.
Harry's grandson will learn good manners as his parents show
him that the world simply does not revolve around their darling
little boy. "Our children add up, imitate, file away what they've
observed," notes child psychiatrist Robert Coles, "and so very
often later fall in line with the particular moral counsel we wit-
tingly or quite unselfconsciously have offered them."[1]

With the help of important adults who make their imprints on
our youthful wet cement,[2] we start in early childhood to sort out
this difficult discernment between fact tattling and truth telling.
Difficult, because it runs contrary to our self-interest. Some of us
learn these lessons more slowly than others. Very, very slowly.
Some of us adults haven't learned the distinction yet.

Chapter Fourteen Study Questions

1. What's the difference between "a fact" and "the truth"?

2. What's the difference between a "fact bearer" and a "truth teller"?

3. Recall an incident from your childhood when you thought you were telling the truth but your parents thought that you should have held your tongue.
   a. What consequences of your "disclosure" did your parents fear?
   b. How did your parents teach you to handle similar situations thereafter?
   c. In retrospect, do you think your parents were right or wrong in silencing you?

4. Keep a list this week of the "truths" that you tell. At the end of the week, review those incidents in light of the five principles for truth telling as opposed to fact tattling. How did you do?

CHAPTER 15

Varnish and Garnish

There are few nudities so objectionable as the naked truth.

Agnes Reppelier, *Compromises*

Above all, my beloved, do not swear, either by heaven or by earth or by any other oath, but let your "Yes" be yes and your "No" be no, so that you may not fall under condemnation.

James 5:12 (NIV)

When I asked Brenda, a young mother of three, what she thought about lying, she answered my question with enthusiasm. "Wow!" she responded, "I can relate to this topic."

Brenda considers herself a very black-and-white person who tells the unvarnished truth regardless of its consequences. She is exceptionally proud of that fact. Since her children have come along, Brenda has been very conscious of the type of example she will set for them. She takes her responsibilities as a parent very seriously. In her lifetime, though, Brenda has gotten herself into plenty of trouble for being so honest. So much so that she occasionally asks herself if the truth is always warranted.

Brenda is about as popular as the child who spoke the truth about the emperor's new clothes while everyone else in the kingdom complimented his naked highness on how well his new wardrobe fit. Her friends may call her blunt, but blunt Brenda is going to keep on telling the truth no matter what. As she sees it,

"If we lie, we really say Satan is our father, since Satan is the father of lies! Truth telling is *so important!*"

David Nyberg, a professor of philosophy and education, thinks that people like Brenda are dangerous. "Is there a moral command that implies a duty to dish out [truth] without garnish to everyone who passes by?" he complains in *The Varnished Truth.*[1] Not only does Nyberg prefer his truth with varnish and garnish, he finds space for untruth in many common life situations. I disagree, but I sympathize with people like Professor Nyberg who have a legitimate complaint with the *effects* of such truth telling.

Are they really human, these people who rigorously devote themselves to telling the truth at all costs—the Brendas, the H. Clay Trumbulls, the Nollie ten Booms? They've made a conscious decision at a personal cost not to let the opinion of others deter them from their fixed standard. In contrast to the average well-intentioned person who wants to lead a decent God-fearing life, they seem to march to a steadier drumbeat than the rest of us who have our honest ups and downs.

I'm grateful to thinkers like Henry Cloud who value truth but can put my concerns into a robust Christian perspective. "Truth without grace is deadly," he warns, "but grace without truth leads to less than successful living as well."[2] Cloud, who has more sympathy than Nyberg has for these single-minded truth tellers, cherishes the virtues that complement truth but do not replace it.

I better understood the tensions in graceless truth myself after an incident last week when I drove to work after a late-winter ice storm.

The woods that flank the winding country road between my house and the highway were eerily beautiful as the morning sun danced off icicles that had coated tree branches during the night. *Snap, crackle, pop.* Like sparks from kindling dancing in a fireplace, this fairyland-beautiful scene sent me a warning about potential danger around the next bend. The weight of the ice had dragged down a tree during the night, pulling live power lines down with it. Thanks to the "beautiful" ice, a tree had fallen, taking with it green promises of what was yet to be.

That's what truth is like without mercy, love, and grace. Beautiful, but dangerous. I see that danger in my friend Mike, a surgeon who prides himself on being truthful with his patients. Is his sort of truthfulness ever warranted?

A few years back, before hospitals banned smoking, I overheard Mike chatting with one of his patients the night before surgery. Nervous about his date with the knife, the patient was in Marlboro country that night. After examining his patient and describing the surgery, Mike took his leave. On the way out the door, he turned ceremoniously and said to his patient, "Oh and by the way, if you keep smoking, you might not wake up from the surgery tomorrow."

Grand finale. Exit doctor, stage left. The patient kept on smoking and fuming.

I have to be honest about my gut response to these rigorous truth tellers. Admire and respect them, yes. Wonder what they have to teach me, certainly. But at some level, they make me nervous. They may not make it onto my list of most preferred saints, but saints they are just the same, and saints sent into my life for a purpose. This is why they make me nervous: I have less difficulty myself in telling the truth than I do in speaking the truth with love. To stand unflinching with the naked truthers would put me at a counterpoint peril to lying.

But there's one arena of life where I, for one, would like to see more unadorned truth.

I started my journal in the final months of an election year. In every newspaper I had access to I read examples of political prevarication from both parties. All the candidates seemed to handle the truth gingerly, as if they might break something. "Truth," said Karl Kraus, "is a clumsy servant that breaks the dishes while washing them."[3] I, for one, would vote for the candidate who broke the most dishes during the campaign.

Dishonesty in government has a big-mouthed silent partner—secrecy, the drug of choice in our nation's capital. Meg Greenfield describes political secrecy as "tempting, addictive and ruinous in the ever-larger doses that are required."[4] Secrecy and cover-ups have replaced the honesty for which early presidents like Washington and Lincoln are remembered.* Within the Washington Beltway, unvarnished, ungarnished truth is warranted indeed.

I did meet one ray of hope this year, a college student majoring in political science who possesses a single-mindedness about truthfulness. I hope Jeremy runs for political office someday, for this young man hasn't told a lie since his freshman year in high school. I believe him when he tells me that, no matter how incredulous his claim may sound:

> In the seventh grade, I learned about my Welsh ancestors and our family motto *Sola Nobilitus Virtus* which means "Virtue alone ennobles." I decided to make it a point not to lie. It was hard and took time but after two years, I reached a point where I told the truth whether people wanted to hear it or not. I don't believe I have told a lie since my freshman year in high school. I used to defend this view by telling people, "My word is my bond," but now, I supplement that with my life verse, James 5:12: "Above all, my beloved, do not swear, either by heaven or by earth or by any other oath, but let your 'Yes' be yes and your 'No' be no, so that you may not fall under condemnation."

Although none of us is called to lie, I believe that some of us are called upon to tell the radical truth. When I reread *The Hiding Place,* I was struck by the almost poetic necessity to hear both sisters' stories. Would we have sensed the conflicts Corrie felt if we had not heard Nollie's dish-breaking story as well? I could not label one sister as right and the other wrong.

---

*Now, at the end of the millennium the American people debate whether it's even important that their president be always truthful.

At crucial moments in world history, someone needs to break so many dishes that we cannot mistake the truth of what we have heard. This special brand of truth teller stands as almost a prophetic figure against the culture. Surely in the public world they will be labeled as absolutists, and the David Nybergs will write books about them. As politicians, they would be that feared fundamentalist that nobody wants to live next door to. But we need these voices in our world. We need public servants whose word is their bond.

On the twenty-fifth anniversary of the Watergate break-in, *Washington Post* editor Ben Bradlee had this advice for our current elected officials: "Stop lying!"[5] No varnish or garnish on Bradlee's words.

Go for it, Jeremy. If you pick up a good working knowledge of economics and foreign affairs to round out your qualifications, you'll have my vote. And I'll pay for any dishes you have to break on your way to the White House.

Chapter Fifteen Study Questions

1. How do you feel about people who apparently are absolutely truthful? Be honest.

2. How important do you think it is to point out other people's faults to them?

3. Recall a time that you told someone the unadorned truth.
   a. What were the consequences?
   b. What happened to your relationship with that person as a result of hearing the truth from you?
   c. Would you handle that disclosure differently today if you had the chance?

4. Which of these three situations most accurately describes the way you would act?
   a. Tell the plain truth no matter what the consequences;
   b. Consider the consequences of the truth you intend to tell and adapt your delivery to fit the situation;
   c. Withhold telling the truth if it didn't feel right.

5. How can your word be your bond?

PART 5

The Language
of the Lie

Language ... often disguises thought.

Alexander Theroux, *Darconville's Cat*

CHAPTER 16

No-Fault Syntax

No-fault syntax is crucially important when issuing vague, no-apology regrets.

John Leo, *"Watch Out for That Language"*

Let no one deceive you with empty words.

Ephesians 5:6 (NIV)

Some years ago I cared for a nine-year-old boy with a deadly brain tumor. I have never known a child with that kind of tumor to survive more than a year. One of my partners had the difficult task of telling his parents the diagnosis and prognosis. This doctor had told them the whole truth and nothing but. I know his style—patient, thorough, compassionate.

Young Kyle went through radiation treatments. With that and the help of steroids, most of his symptoms went away. About a month after the treatment ended, I repeated the MRI to see where things stood. The pattern of black and white and gray said that nothing had changed. How much nicer it would have been if all the sinister shadows had disappeared, if only for a little while. How, I wondered, would I tell the family this?

Kyle was in the room when his mother asked the results. "I have some good news," I told her. "The tumor has not progressed." Well, my hopeful spin was true—half true. Neither had it gone away, but she inquired no further.

That evening Kyle's mother and I were guests on a local television talk show. Kyle was there too, sitting between us in a spiffy, three-piece vested suit. At the end of the interview, his mother said directly to the camera, "I have to tell you what happened today. Today Dr. Komp told me that my baby is going to be okay. There was another doctor we called 'Dr. Gloom and Doom,' but Dr. Komp told me my son would be okay."

How could I correct her in front of her son, in front of the television audience? I smiled weakly, regretting that I had so softened the news that she had drawn that incorrect conclusion.

When Kyle died, the family did fine, even with the less euphemistic doctor they called "Gloom and Doom." But I've been thinking about my choice of words ever since.

There's so much bad news in this world that seems to beg to be softened, especially in the field of medicine. This textual softening-up process intends to console the hearer, but more often it comforts the euphemizer rather than the euphemizee.

Euphemizing risks the dissolution of the truth, and sometimes it covers up danger.

One morning in Chicago I set off early from my hotel to mail a package and met two friendly police officers standing on the street corner. I asked them if there was a post office nearby.

"Whew!" said one cop, shaking his head. "Not around here."

"Where's the nearest post office?" I wondered, looking to his partner who might be more informative.

"Not within walking distance," his partner answered. "About six blocks that way," he said, waving his hand in a direction somewhat vaguely south.

"Not within walking distance," both officers repeated. "UPS will be open at 10:00 A.M. Why don't you just wait?"

Why wait when six blocks is not too far to walk? Having the time and needing the exercise, I set off past handsome banners that proclaimed "Illinois Medical District." The flags pointed to the illuminated, crisp medical towers of South Ashland's Bedpan Alley.

There were many churches along my route to the post office. Bullet-shaped holes marred the simple glass cross on a Lutheran

house of worship. A sign was broken off another church, but her
boarded doors still proclaimed her watchword: "As for me and
my house, we will serve the Lord." Hard to serve God on South
Ashland, it would seem. Hard to come within walking distance.

My path took me down the streets of Cook County Hospital's encatchment area. "Encatchment area"—that's medspeak
for the 'hood that fills the bedpans of this Chicago Hope. When
I was a young doctor, Cook County had 3,000 active beds. Today
less than 500 beds remain open for the sick of South Ashland
who are sicker now than they have ever been before. I wondered
whether visiting nurses need police escorts here as they do in the
neighborhood that surrounds New Haven's Pill Hill where I
work. Not easy to serve those who have been managed-cared out
of those 2,500 other beds.

"Not within walking distance" was the policeman's way of
saying to me "you shouldn't walk there." But the people who
live on South Ashland walk there every day. As I strolled past an
old brownstone house on that nippy autumn day, a working girl
in stilettoed heels and micro-miniskirt shouted final instructions
to her latchkey son before moving towards a shiny new Lincoln
Town Car blasting gangsta rap music at the curb. The people of
South Ashland live within walking distance of poverty and pros-
titution and crime.

"Not within walking distance" is a way we can use words to
stand at a distance from truth, when truth is too uncomfortable.
A euphemism is one way, but there are other wordy ways to sep-
arate ourselves from that which is truthful but painful.

In the fertile fields of euphemism known as hospitals, highly
active intellects sink into literal passivity to complete the detox-
ification process that the euphemism began. Although lies might
be detected, no one would lie. "Say there was dissimulation and
people won't think you're terrible," quipped one woman, "but if
you say that you lied, then you are scum." With euphemisms and
passive voice, it's nobody's fault. "No-fault syntax," says John

Leo, "is crucially important when issuing vague, no-apology regrets."[1] But has anybody heard the truth?

We don't slice our hospital budgets these days. We participate in "patient-focused, operational redesign." Patients don't die in our midst. They just expire. Following their expiration, we don't send them to the morgue. We discharge them to Brady. A dead body isn't a corpse either. It is the remains unless, of course, it is cremated, in which case it becomes a "cremains." And in Holland these days, doctors do not discuss euthanasia with their patients. Instead, they "take the initiative to create an opportunity for patients to discuss their wishes concerning the end of life."[2] One man's death with dignity becomes another woman's final exit.

I like what Hannah More said about precision with words. "Let us fortify our virtue by calling things by their proper names."[3]

These days as I reach out to find a merciful version of the truth, I am reinforcing my integrity with a more careful and precise choice of words.

How about you?

Chapter Sixteen Study Questions

1. Do you have any pet phrases you use to discuss embarrassing or painful subjects? (Death, sex, body functions, and religion are good places to look.) Make a list of alternative ways to express the same idea.

2. Recall a euphemism that someone told you that misled you. How would you rephrase that so that you heard the truth gently and clearly?

3. Read back through your journal and find examples of euphemisms that you have used.

CHAPTER 17

Jihad Journalism

The problem with such Old Testament journalism
is getting the God's-eye view right.

Tim Stafford,
"Show Biz Reporters and Jihad Journalism"

Do not slander one another.

James 4:11 (NIV)

Most lies are like the virtual mutt who gets into mischief on my computer screen every time I stop typing for a few minutes. I pause for an idea-break, and my screen saver, Bad Dog™, enters stage right to dig up my screenscape. Bad Dog's creators claim that he "messes up your life without changing the course of history."

That's the impact of most untruthfulness in ordinary life—messy but not momentous. On the other hand, lies like slander and libel have profound and devastating impact.

Slander changed the course of history for a man named Sylvester Turner. "A lie if left unchallenged," Turner lamented in the libel suit he brought to recover his damaged reputation, "becomes the truth."

Almost on the eve of a Houston mayoral election, KTRK-TV reported that candidate Turner may have participated in a fraud perpetrated by one of his clients. After reporter Wayne Dolcefino aired his investigative report, Turner called a press conference to deny the charges. Even the judge in the fraud case stated publicly that Turner was not under investigation. Although KTRK had a reporter on hand for each of these denials, the station failed to air the coverage that contradicted their hot story and favored Turner.

Turner, who was ahead in the polls before Dolcefino's program aired, lost the election. In the street, KTRK viewers stopped the Harvard Law School graduate, who had hoped to be Houston's first African-American mayor, to ask him why he was not in jail. Where there is smoke there must be fire, right?

Court TV anchor Gregg Garrett called Turner's suit "a trial about truth and lies in a Texas courtroom." Questioned by his own lawyer, Wayne Dolcefino sounded more like a hotshot reporter on the trail of a righteous story than a malicious man trying to bring down a political candidate. Yet videotapes showed Dolcefino appearing to hound a potential witness who was dying of AIDS in an attempt to get the goods on Turner.

Two very different images emerged under questioning by the plaintiff's and defendant's lawyers, leading to two very different possible conclusions about the truth of the matter. Garrett's colleague Clara Tuma commented, "The lawyers say one thing and reality is another."

Dolcefino's point of view: The witness gives evidence that the plaintiff was involved in the fraud up to his eyeballs. Turner's contention: Dolcefino depended on a witness who had previously perjured himself and now admits it. Furthermore, there were innuendoes that Dolcefino may have purchased the damning testimony.

On the summing-up day there was TV starpower on hand to hear a Texas-style duel that resembled a barroom brawl more than a courtroom proceeding. KTRK's superstars showed up in Texas-sized numbers to lend their halo effect to their comrade. Even the vastly popular weatherman was on hand.

Which version of the story was the truth? In the end, the jury believed Sylvester Turner and awarded him $5,500,000. But were they able to give him back his reputation for which he came to court?

Objective reporting makes a tremendous difference to an authentic lover of truth. In our society, investigative reporting can hold candidates and others in authority accountable to the people they serve. Note, I said "can."

Contaminating the reporting pool are "jihad journalists" who simply seek verification of their own slanted points of view. Blinded by the cause that began their holy war, they no longer seek the whole truth. They think they already know the truth and scout around only for snappy quotations that support their foregone conclusions. They stop investigating and start stalking. Claiming to serve truth, they promote falsehood.

While to my knowledge no one has ever slandered me, misquotation by the media has mightily disturbed me. Some journalists are so intent on proving their point that they do not rightly hear what I have to say. Twice in the last year I have written letters to the editor to correct misquotation stemming from editorial bias. Both times the magazines honored my request to respond in print, but if they had gotten their facts straight the first time around, there would have been less damage. I am still dealing with the fallout from readers who saw the original articles, but never saw the editorial apologies.

But there is something worse than journalists misquoting during an interview. When we as readers overexpose ourselves to biased journalism, we begin to prejudge situations in our own lives. We justify our own pet causes as "on the side of truth," sometimes to the point of slander. We may not end up in court because of careless untruthful words, but we can change the course of history.

Few of us are journalists, but all of us have opinions. And we love to hear juicy stories. "How long will you assail a person?" the psalmist asks you and me about our gossip, as much as he indicts libelous journalists. "Will you batter your victim, all of you, as you would a leaning wall, a tottering fence? Their only plan is to bring down a person of prominence. They take pleasure in falsehood; they bless with their mouths, but inwardly they curse" (Psalm 62:3–4 NRSV).

A teen friend of mine asked for my help with a situation she ran into in school. In her opinion, the pastor of another church was guilty of "child abuse" because he had criticized a young friend of hers. Kathy wanted her own pastor to ride out on his white charger and rescue her chum.

In the process, Kathy had not considered the accused pastor's side of the story. Neither had she thought about the possible effect of a slanderous false accusation on this pastor's reputation, especially under the emotionally charged rubric of "child abuse."

If lying is defined as communication with the intention to deceive, most of our own gossip falls short of qualifying as bald-faced lies. In repeating allegations that we cannot substantiate, we lie to ourselves, if not knowingly to the one whom we tell:

We deceive ourselves that it is any of our business in the first place.

We deceive ourselves that we have followed scriptural guidelines for dealing with the faults of others.

"Once a newspaper touches a story," said Norman Mailer, "the facts are lost forever, even to the protagonists."[1] The same is true about gossip. Once gossip touches a story, the facts are lost forever, especially for those who like the particular version that they have heard. When we fail to get all the facts but speak nonetheless, we serve falsehood. When we take pleasure in repeating "facts" that we cannot substantiate, we speak slander. The apostle James explains it best:

- Be quick to listen, slow to speak (1:19).
- If any think they are religious, and do not bridle their tongues but deceive their hearts, their religion is worthless (1:26).
- Do not speak evil against one another (4:11).

I want to give you a postscript to those letters to the editor that I wrote. The first time, I contacted the magazine editor, concerned that the writer who interviewed me had misquoted me. The editor agreed to publish my letter, but I asked him whether out of courtesy I should speak with the writer as well. The editor reassured me that I had fulfilled any ethical requirement by contacting him. After my letter was published, though, the writer contacted me.

The manuscript he turned in to the magazine had carefully expressed my opinions correctly, but my letter to the editor implied that he was responsible for the misquotation. He sent me copies of his correspondence with the editor to prove his point. The changes had occurred in the editorial process, but my letter put the writer in a bad light. Although I did not intend to deceive, my letter was nonetheless untrue. I did not have my facts straight. My investigation had not been thorough enough. Neither was my verbal apology to that writer adequate to undo any slurs on his reputation that someone who read my letter to the editor might have garnered. The same magazine declined to let me respond or apologize to him in print. My statement and the magazine's apology to me stood as the last words.

James has some further observations about the carefulness of our words as Christians:

- When we slander or judge another, we speak against the law and judge the law (4:11).
- When we grumble about another, the "Judge is standing at the door" waiting to judge us (5:9).

When the second misquotation happened, I followed a different approach that exceeds the normal ethic of journalism but makes good Christian sense to me. Before I contacted the editor, I called the writer. He refused to retract what he had said in print, but his editor agreed to print a letter from me to which they would make an editorial response.

Which episode do I find more satisfying? To tell you the truth, I am more at peace about the second, despite the fact that I did not have the last word in print and despite disagreement with some of the things the editor and writer said in their response. In the end, what mattered was how I behaved. I like Peter's advice in this regard: "Keep a clear conscience, so that those who speak maliciously against your good behavior in Christ may be ashamed of their slander" (1 Peter 3:16 NIV).

"Why is gossip like a three-pronged tongue?" asks the Babylonian Talmud. "Because it destroys three people: the person who says it, the person who listens to it, and the person about whom it is told." Let's keep our own reporting straight. Let us not destroy.

Chapter Seventeen Study Questions

1. What did you read in a newspaper or see on television this week that has to do with truth telling?

2. When you hear or read a sensational story, how do you determine whether or not to believe it?

3. Read an expose-type article in a newspaper or magazine. Make a list of potential impacts that the story may have on the subject of the report.

4. Recall "broadcasting" a story about someone else.
    a. Did any facts come to your attention later that changed your interpretation of the event?
    b. Did that gossip destroy anyone or a relationship with someone?

5. Name some ways you can become accountable for your own words.

CHAPTER 18

From Borrowed Feathers
to Stolen Words

No, [plagiarism] isn't murder. But like murder it
intrigues us at a comfortable remove, when we're
out of the line of fire and have been excused from
the jury.

Thomas Mallon,
*Stolen Words: Forays Into
the Origins and Ravages of Plagiarism*

"Therefore," declares the LORD, "I am against the
prophets who steal from one another words sup-
posedly from me."

Jeremiah 23:30 (NIV)

A college student friend of mine showed me a trick on the Internet. Without much effort, you can find (and buy) a term paper
on almost any subject. So commonplace has the practice of plagiarism become that many students don't even stop to think of
the morality involved. So commonplace has the practice become
on college campuses that schools are returning to honor codes
with harsh penalties for the lie of claiming someone else's handsomely turned phrase as your own. Perhaps, if plagiarism were
not so common in the literary world, students would not think
that it is a minor offense.

All ideas may belong to the universe, but in our society the
ways in which we express them belong to the person who says

it first. There has been a legal "ownership" for unique expressions ever since the printing press made livelihood possible and originality a priority for writers.

A famous author once lamented: "Sometimes I think I ought to stop writing altogether since I cannot tell surely which of my ideas are borrowed feathers."[1] With that regret, Helen Keller responded to her second—not her first—accusation of plagiarism. Perhaps the famous blind author's case would have been better served if the charming metaphor of "borrowed feathers" had been her own. Long before Keller responded to the accusations of plagiarism, Aesop had used the phrase in "The Jay and the Peacock." You might know the punch line to that fable: "It is not only fine feathers that make fine birds."

In some way, we have all participated in this form of borrowing. Every student with a paper due tomorrow knows the temptation to lift a few succulent passages from someone else with a cleverer mind. Plagiarism did not take on the nature of crime until books made it possible for writers to earn a living by their printed wit.

Even so, it takes more than neatly turned phrases to make a great writer and more than profound punditry to make a student passable or a professor worthy of tenure. Clever word-birds need morals too. But oh, how our ethics slip when we fall in love with someone else's elegant plumes! Implied in the textual theft is a compliment of sorts. But even a thief who does homage is a pirate all the same.

After he was charged with plagiarism, one dazzlingly brilliant, but impossibly vain author issued a letter of apology to his victim. He offered his congratulations that the plagiarizer might have mistaken his victim's words for his very own. But it's not a joke; it's a plague. Some contemporary writers lie numerous times about the originality of their work, and then call it a disease—an addiction.

A best-selling novelist recently announced her entry into therapy to tame her obsession with a rival's bon mots. Past performances of literary codependents predict that she, alas, will fall off the word wagon and once again imbibe at another novelist's well.

What is most remarkable about this is how talented all these plagiarizing authors are without help from anyone else. It hardly seems worth the risk to phrase filch from others. Even more astounding is the paper trail that chronic plagiarizers inevitably leave behind. How, you may ask, can the highly educated not really know when cunningly phrased passages are not their own? Aren't these amongst the easiest of lies to detect? The italics in the following selection indicate exact duplication by Helen Keller of another author's previously published work:

> We were especially happy when the trees began to put on their autumn robes. Oh, yes! I could imagine how beautiful the trees were, all aglow, and rustling in the sunlight. *We thought the leaves as pretty as flowers, and carried great bunches home to mother. The golden leaves I called buttercups and the red ones roses.* One day teacher said, "Yes, they are *beautiful enough to comfort us for the flight of summer.*"[2]

I must admit that as careful as I have been to honor other authors in all my writing, and as especially careful as I have been in this book about truthfulness to be honest, the admiration for a fellow writer's pretty plumage can be a mighty powerful craving. Perhaps you've read something and said to yourself, or even to others, "I wish I had said that first!" In his book *Stolen Words,* Thomas Mallon cites an old authors' joke: "I wish I'd said that, Jimmy," sighs Oscar. "Don't worry, Oscar," comes the reply. "You will."[3]

Last month a journalist told me about interviews he conducted for a magazine article. After his first draft had been prepared, he found an even better source than his earlier ones. When the revised article was complete, he shared it with all his sources to make sure that he was quoting them accurately and in proper context. To my friend's dismay, his new source found his own published words in the article, attributed to someone else. This discouraged journalist later said to me, "I guess the ultimate ethical question is, 'What principles will you put aside for a good quote?'"

When faced with a wonderful phrase by a misplaced or unknown author, a careful writer will footnote that, inviting readers to supply the missing credit and including any acknowledgment uncovered in subsequent editions.

A recently published story shows just how far someone might go for quotation without attribution. In his autobiography *Leading With My Chin,* Jay Leno sinks to a new level of legalized deception. Leno tells an embarrassing story about an event on the *Dinah Shore Show* many years ago. But this incident never happened to Leno.

The comedian, it appears, liked the story so much that he paid the person to whom it happened $1,000 for the right to publish the peccadillo as his own. Although his payment spares Leno from any legal charges, his plagiarism of a life illustrates how little respect our cultural icons have for the unvarnished truth.

US News & World Report columnist John Leo called for Jay Leno to revise his autobiography and remove anything that didn't actually happen to him. "The best antidote," writes Leo about this disregard for truthfulness by people in public life, "is to care about the truth . . . and to teach respect for truth in our schools."[4]

John Leo, not Jay Leno, is absolutely right. "Even tiny fibs matter." Even the charming and pretty ones.

Perhaps all communicators would do well to heed the advice given another Aesop peacock who envied the nightingale's voice: "Be content with your lot; one cannot be first in everything."

Chapter Eighteen Study Questions

1. When you were a student, did you ever present someone else's work as your own? Looking back, why do you think you did that?

2. How does plagiarism violate the commandment not to bear false witness against our neighbors?

3. In the context of your spoken and written words, who is your "neighbor" whose belongings you shouldn't covet?

PART 6

Honest Hearts

In order to swim one takes off all one's clothes—in order to aspire to the truth one must undress in a far more inward sense, divest oneself of all one's inward clothes, of thoughts, conceptions, selfishness, etcetera before one is sufficiently naked.

Søren Kierkegaard, *Journals*

CHAPTER 19

Dented Discipline

It is not the whip that makes us, but the lure of things that are worthy to be loved.

Woodrow Wilson

God opposes the proud but gives grace to the humble.

1 Peter 5:5 (NIV)

This morning when I tanked up at the gas station, I saw the first scratch in my handsome new Legacy's body. So minor a blemish would have gone unnoticed on my old car, lost among all its multi-mini-dents. But my romance with this new chariot is still at the stage where every peewee pockmark is a grand calamity. This sleek new beauty replaced a beat-up heap of antiquity. Some time after my old car's fifth birthday, I stopped repairing every parking lot mishap lest my insurance premiums skyrocket into outer space. By the time that car and I parted company, it looked somewhat unkempt and underloved.

When I got home from the filling station, I rubbed the new car's coat back to Spruce Green perfection. Well, I thought, at least we made it through four months without a scratch. Is that the way this discipline about truth telling will end up, I wondered, with one dent after another until I don't care anymore?

Has it not been that way with every other project in my life? Early on in my projects, I pay attention to small failures and restore perfection before much damage is done. Like the diet to end all diets in 1990. That time I paid great attention to every gram of fat that went in my mouth and engaged in an exercise program that would have exhausted a woman half my age. By my fiftieth birthday, I fit back into a size nine dress. But as I face sixty, I must begin the birthday preparations again with a body that looks more like my old car than the new.

I started this journey toward a higher standard of truthfulness the same way I start any new project: with great vigor, a gusty sprint rather than a measured mile. As long as I pay strict attention to discipline, I'm perfect. I am in control. But eventually I slide back into old patterns. The last few days I've noticed that exaggeration and some little white lies have busted out all over again. I didn't even write them down in my journal. Can I ever whip myself into admirably truthful shape? I wonder.

But it's not the whip that makes us. What makes us is the lure of things that are worthy to be loved. You will become the truth teller you really want to be when you begin to love the truth, which is different from the love of *being* truthful. Will loving the truth mean you will always tell the truth? Possibly not. But it will be the love of truth—not rugged self-discipline—that will turn you into a truthful person.

Nineteen chapters ago, you and Babu and I started this journey with an embarrassing lesson about my pride. A year later, and with Babu nestled comfortably by my side, I come to you a more consistently truthful person but still suffering from an overdose of pride. It is pride, after all, that prevents most of us from telling the truth. Love rejoices with the truth. But what use is love, said Abba Elias, when there is pride?[1]

Seventh-century Christian John Climacus found a strong inverse link between truth and pride. To Climacus, pride was a certain sign of barrenness, the mother of condemnation, the harbinger of madness, the author of downfall, a flight from God's sure and steadfast help.[2] Where pride rules, neither truth nor love has a fighting chance.

If I had to graph my journey toward truthfulness, it would resemble a roller coaster that runs from earth to heaven. Sometimes I'm up, sometimes I'm down, oh yes, Lord! Sound familiar? My hunch is that your own journey could be graphed very much like mine, and that you react to a roller-coaster ride the same way I do.

On the trip down, I tend to beat up on myself and resent the fact that I'm just not moving onward and upward towards complete honesty. If I were really spiritual, I tell myself, I would not be taking these excursions back down. But here's the good news:

Each trip down teaches me something that I can use on the return trip to the high points.

With that trip down comes the conviction that I don't want to go down as low as I've gone in the past.

During that trip down comes the assurance that I will not go down as low as I've gone in the past.

Even with my ups and downs, my eventual goal remains the same.

All those dents in my discipline, all those downhill rides, teach me that the object of the exercise was not to become perfectly truthful so that I could be proud of my truthfulness. The goal was to be truthful out of love for God and my fellow beings. That's the lure of love that buoys me back up.

On one of those trips down, I grasped what Climacus meant about the healing of pride: "Men can heal the lustful. Angels can heal the malicious. Only God can heal the proud."[3]

I want to be truthful. But I also want to be whole.

Chapter Nineteen Study Questions

1. Look back through your journal and find examples of lies you told that were to protect your pride. What aspect of yourself were you trying to protect?

2. What did you have to say to yourself in your journal after you slipped up? Did you stop journaling for a while? Why?

3. In your journal, how did you discriminate between conviction and self-condemnation?

CHAPTER 20

Read My Lips

He's a liar born, and he'll die a liar. Look at his face; ain't it written there? Let him turn those eyes of his on me. I defy him to do it.

Charles Dickens, *Great Expectations*

He winketh with his eyes, he speaketh with his feet, he teacheth with his fingers.

Proverbs 6:13 (KJV)

On my office wall at Yale there's a painting of boys and girls flying kites on a warm summer day. So special is this canvas that it became the cover design for my first book.[1] When the twelve-year-old artist finished this painting, she was very pleased with what she had accomplished. But Korey was so serious about her artwork that she wanted truthful, not inflated praise. Believing that doctors (and other adults) don't always necessarily tell the truth, the child devised her own informal polygraph test to examine my heart.

Korey finished the painting the night before she had surgery for bone cancer. She knew that she would be in the operating room under anesthesia when I first saw her masterpiece, and that worried her a bit. Before they left home for the hospital that morning, she gave her parents strict instructions.

"When Dr. Komp opens the package, look at her eyes. She may say that she likes it, but I want to know what she really thinks."

Korey's comment struck me at first as humorous, then as disturbing. Was it doctors specifically or adults in general that she didn't trust to always speak the truth with their lips? Or was it me, whose intention is to always be truthful, that she didn't trust? Whichever, the child knew that we are capable of lying when we don't take people seriously.

In Korey's statement I heard inverse echoes of a colleague who sat in that same office, listening to a scathing critique I gave a lazy student. When the young man left my office, this doctor friend told me, "Di, I don't think he heard a word you said." I thought I had made myself perfectly clear. "Perhaps he would have understood what you were really saying if he knew you better and knew that you never lose your temper, even when you should. Since you controlled how angry you felt, he left here thinking there wasn't much wrong."

Looking back now, I realize that my friend was right. When listening for the truth, most of the world counts on both lips and eyes to say the same thing. Anything less communicative risks either falsehood or at least deception. We can't have "no, no" on our lips and "yes, yes" in our eyes and tell the truth.

In his best-selling anthem in praise of cyberlife,[2] Bill Gates extols the virtues of a very different world from the one in which Korey would be able to judge truthfulness. The Microsoft billionaire marvels at the idea of a virtual village where we can judge a person only by the text they offer. Gates even worries about a new technological advancement called "video enhancement" that will allow cybernauts to see the person with whom they're chatting.

Alas, as Doug Groothuis points out, Gates mistakes connectivity for community. Genuine community, Groothuis says, "shines through the human presence of truth expressed personally."[3] Unlike connectivity, community is a place where we have the opportunity not only to hear truth but to see it as well.

This potential mismatch of lips and eyes, the incongruence of head and heart, is something that we humans have been dealing with throughout our history. Most of us use more than one way to "talk." Indirectly we have been visiting this concept all through this book. Here are some reminders of body language from earlier chapters:

- "Only as Corrie ten Boom walked out of the army building after lying did she begin to tremble" (chapter 3).
- ". . . smiling women with smiling hearts, and smiling women with unseen broken hearts" (chapter 4).
- "One of the things we women doctors learn early in our medical education is to put away our tears, even when the heart's honest response would have been to cry" (chapter 4).
- "Other women took off their smiley masks as well, and we all were healed as we listened to each other's true stories" (chapter 4).
- "Fletcher Reede smiled convincingly through each of his lies" (chapter 13).

Body language is a vital tool to anyone interested in discerning the truth. Do you remember the story of Shiprah and Puah? Stop and think about how you "saw" their stories as I retold them. I suspect that you not only "listened" to their stories in the text but also pictured the participants with your mind's eye. What was it that you "saw"?

Think of the consequences on all the lives concerned if the women's body language had told a different story than their words. Moses, for one, would not have survived. Similarly, if Rahab had not been able to control her nonverbal communication about the spies' location in Jericho, Joshua would not have entered the Promised Land that particular day.

Watch a lawyer observing a jury and you'll see a ballet of body language in motion. And watch jurors study the body language of the defendant at the same time they carefully control their own body language so that no one in the courtroom can possibly read their minds. But heaven help the witness who doesn't display emotion ever so slightly! No one seems to know how to discern truth when all they've got is a stranger's words. The police know this too.[4]

Of all the different types of professionals I've talked with in the last years, the most tortured about truthfulness on the job have been police officers. Doctors, lawyers, and pastors struggle with truthfulness because their own human nature impacts their work ethic. Basically, all three types of professionals are supposed to tell the truth. The police, on the other hand, have deception built into their job descriptions at the same time they are working hard to determine if someone else is telling the truth.

One of the most interesting books I have read is Don Rabon's text for police officers, *Interviewing and Interrogation*. I was encouraged to learn that the Chairman of the Law Enforcement Department of the North Carolina Justice Academy is so deeply conscious of the role of ethics and faith in his professional life. In his chapters on deceptive techniques, Rabon asks the police to "consider using deception only as a last resort after exploring—but not succeeding with—all of the truthful persuasive approaches in those circumstances."[5] Like my young friend Korey, Rabon believes that the eyes are windows to the soul.[6] But even eyes can learn to deceive.

We depend on body language because we distrust so much of what people have to say. Children and teenagers are rarely accomplished enough to carry off complete deceit. It takes years of experience to bring our subconscious language into conscious control. I suspect that one of the reasons we think that teenagers lie more often than adults is that teenagers have not yet mastered this double duplicity.

By the time we're adults, we dress up this form of deception and call it our right to private thoughts. Fair enough, if we choose to say nothing. But think about those times that we do speak out. Is it fair to deliberately disguise the feelings that accompany our words?

Only an accomplished and committed liar can perfectly control body language. But some pundits are advising the street-smart, successful businessperson to work on it. You can learn these tricks in *What They Don't Teach You at Harvard Business School*.[7] The author recommends that we seek control over the nonverbal clues we transmit to others.

I guess I'm not very street-smart, because I allow my wardrobe to gossip about me. The book says that instead of the flashy prints I favor, I should wear dark-colored power suits. That way I can create a nonrevelatory impression and, at the same time, carefully study the expressive wardrobe and body language of the person across the desk from me.

I think our Yale-New Haven Hospital intern wannabes read that book this year before they came for their interviews. Even our women applicants look more like candidates for the FBI Academy this year than our next class of pediatric residents. They look kind of nice so neatly dressed, but they all look alike. I wish they had packed themselves in their suitcases instead of these business-smart uniforms. Next year, when they are wearing surgical scrubs and take out their contact lenses for another all-nighter, I'll meet the real them. Sleep deprivation has a way of flushing out the truthful body language. Ask the police.

I'm not signing up for video enhancement for my computer yet. Neither will I take McCormack's advice about my wardrobe. My patients and my friends need to see and feel me with their eyes and their ears and souls. Rather than an FBI suit for work, I would rather wear my black-and-white patchwork sweater, with swatches of rabbit fur quilted in. My little patients love this sweater, for the bunny bits are an invitation to touch my words with their hearts.

Most of all, I need to give some serious thought to the way I've mastered control of my emotive body language. I would never want the Koreys in my life to lose confidence that they could judge when their doctor and friend is telling them the truth.

Chapter Twenty Questions

1. On a scale of 1 to 10, how much do you depend on body language to interpret someone's claim to be truth telling?

2. What signs of body language do you rely on most?

3. Recall an experience when body language helped you discern the truth correctly.

4. Recall an experience when you were misled by body language and misjudged someone's words.

5. Give an example of someone you've encountered from a different culture whose use of body language is entirely different from your own.

6. Would you describe yourself as a very open person or someone who is guarded?

7. In your experience, are open people or guarded people more honest? Why?

CHAPTER 21

Hearing the Truth
with Courage

It takes two to speak the truth—one to speak and
another to hear.

Henry David Thoreau,
A Week on the Concord and Merrimack Rivers

He who has an ear, let him hear.

Revelation 13:9 (NIV)

As I prepared for a doctor's appointment where *I* was the
patient I learned firsthand that even adults fear that punishment follows truthfulness. Psychologists call this denial. Listen
to this story and see what you would call it.

A questionnaire sat on my desk at home, incomplete, waiting
for me to fill in the blanks before I went in for a medical test.
Sounds silly, writing it down this way, not unlike a teenager facing her parents on report card day. I hesitated to complete the
questionnaire because I didn't want to tell my doctor that I didn't
practice what I preached. The blanks remained blank because I
didn't want to hear the inevitable lecture that would follow truthful answers to the questions.

"How many servings of dairy products do you consume in
an average day?" the questionnaire asks. Well, I know what the
"right" answer is supposed to be for a woman my age. I'm a doctor, after all, so I can't plead ignorance. But there's no milk or

yogurt in my refrigerator right now. Didn't go shopping on the way home from work tonight. Too tired. Not a good day to be filling this out.

"Please list all your current medications including vitamins and calcium." Ugh, how I hate those megamonsters. Hard to swallow. I buy the pills all right, but the bottles sit unopened on my bathroom shelf.

Right about now I feel like a three-year-old caught with both hands in the cookie jar, but a brilliant resolution enters my mind. What if I were to postpone the bone density test for a few months and start on a proper regimen of dairy products, vitamins, and Tums 500™? I could turn over a new leaf—preferably calcium-rich green—and then reschedule the test when I can answer honestly that I've done all the right things. My bones may not be denser, but at least I can give the right answers. The questionnaire, after all, doesn't ask how long I've been living healthy.

"Patients tell doctors less than they know," says David Nyberg, "doctors tell patients more than they know; and both seem to want it this way."[1] I don't agree with much else in Nyberg's book *The Varnished Truth,* but this time his finger is right on the problem's pulse. "We—both the patients and the doctors—are inclined to deny this, as well as the further accusation that we lie to ourselves on purpose to get what we want, in order to save face. The source of this denial runs deep."[2]

It's humiliating to come to terms with the fact that I am no better than the most noncompliant of my patients. "Why would she lie to a doctor?" I stormed when I caught Petra in a lie. "I'm only here to help her. The only person she hurt by that lie is herself."

Do you remember what Michael Josephson said about our little white lies? (chapter 4). I'd like to convince myself that the only person who could be hurt by less than truthful answers on the questionnaire is myself, but this time I know for a fact that it simply is not true.

The questions weren't constructed as a booby trap for non-compliant patients. The doctor who is analyzing bone density results is putting my answers together with those of many other middle-aged women. When he collates the results, he'll draw conclusions about the impact of all these lifestyle factors on bone strength in later life. If his results are reliable, women will receive sound advice. If the answers are inflated, the beneficial effects of those factors will be minimized.

Josephson was right. Little white lies plant land mines for neighbors.

Why would a patient not want to hear the truth from a doctor? Or worse yet, why would a patient lie? For the same reasons that children fib to their parents about their problems at school: to escape a lecture. Translate that: to escape punishment and humiliation. There aren't many doctors who offer unconditional love. I want my doctor to think of me as the perfect patient, and that's what some of the parents in my practice expect from me.

I have a mother's face in mind as I write. What a character Amy was—she still is! It wasn't easy for me to shepherd her daughter through treatment for a brain tumor a decade ago. Amy was always polite to me, but could that mom ever get into mischief when I let her loose in a different part of the hospital! Radiology technicians reported foul-mouthed abuse. The pharmacist never wanted to see her again. Amy didn't seem to understand that they were only trying to help her little girl. Why couldn't she just listen and trust?

I can see the examining room where we sat the day her boyfriend gently coaxed her to tell me the truth. Both of their faces are so clear in my mind. "I signed myself into a rehab program last month," Amy confessed. "That's why I missed the last appointment. I have serious problems with both alcohol and prescription medications."

Since I had chalked her misadventures up to personality, I never had suspected that there was anything more to it. But now

Amy was courageously hearing and speaking the truth about a serious problem that was planting land mines for her children.

"I can't believe you never suspected," she tells me, shaking her head. I search my memory for clues and find none. "Though I must admit," Amy continues, "that I was always careful around you. I didn't want you to think bad of me. If I was drunk or stoned, I missed an appointment rather than let you see me that way."

I was dumbfounded. Am I so judgmental that Amy couldn't afford to tell the truth to someone she liked and respected? What was she afraid to hear from my lips or see in my eyes?

"Why don't we try this in the future," I told Amy. "If you take a deep breath and risk telling me the truth, I'll take a deep breath and listen to you with love. Think that would work?" It did, or at least it worked until I went on sabbatical and another doctor took over her daughter's care for the year.

Fortunately, the child had already completed chemo by the time Amy went AWOL after her first appointment with him. The covering doctor made the mistake of matching wills with Amy's equally iron one. He sent a certified registered letter to her house warning what steps he might take if she continued to miss appointments.

Amy called our secretary. "That letter at the post office, is that from you? I'm not going to pick it up!"

My secretary told me this story when I came back from Germany. I had a sly grin on my face when I said, "I'm going to send Amy a letter that she's going to open. Furthermore, she'll call in promptly for an appointment." No one could imagine how I could get Amy to return.

On a small plain envelope, I wrote out her name by hand— "Amy West Anderson North"—and then her address. I chose a fancy stamp popular with teenagers that year, placed the stamped envelope in a larger envelope, and mailed it to a friend in Cleveland for him to post from there. A week later, my secretary got a call from Amy.

"See you on Monday!" Amy said, laughing. Unbelieving, my secretary asked her how I lured her to open the letter.

"It drove me crazy when I got this letter that looked like it was from a kid. It was postmarked from Cleveland and addressed to my maiden name, my ex-husband's name, and my boyfriend's name," she laughed. "I didn't recognize the handwriting. And who in Cleveland would know my whole life's history and the fathers of all my children? Nobody outside the family I could think of. So I opened it."

"What did Dr. Komp write in the letter that you were willing to make the appointment?" my secretary persisted.

"There were only two sentences and her signature."

To my prodigal I had written: "The coast is clear. Lassie come home."

And what about this prodigal middle-aged doctor? Chances are my doctor won't be as clever as I was with Amy. He may even think that an adult should act like an adult! I guess it's up to me to take a deep breath and hear the truth with courage.

I returned to the questionnaire and continued to read. "Do you exercise regularly?" the page persisted unrelentingly.

I filled in the blanks with ink so that I could not erase my answers later and replace them with a clever lie. "Unfortunately, no," I wrote bravely, "but thanks for the healthy reminder."

I think I am ready to listen.

Chapter Twenty-One Study Questions

1. How would you define "denial"?

2. Think of a time in your life it took you a long time to hear the truth. List the reasons you think you couldn't hear it the first time.

3. Which of the following do you think you would use to help someone else courageously hear the truth? Cross through those that you would not use.
   a. Tell it like it is so that there's no mistake what the truth is.
   b. Build up a trusting relationship with that person first.
   c. Share a story from my own life that illustrates how I have handled a similar situation.

4. If your boss offered to frankly tell you how he or she feels about you and assured you that it will have no effect on your working relationship or your employment record, would you take your boss up on the offer? Why do you think you would decide the way you did?

5. Have you ever lied to your doctor? Why do you think you did that?

6. If you are overdue to see your doctor because you're afraid of what you might learn, make a plan to help you hear the truth with courage.

CHAPTER 22

Speaking the Truth
in Love

Speaking the truth in love, we must *grow up* in
every way into him who is the head, into Christ.

Ephesians 4:15 (NRSV, italics mine)

To preach the Gospel is not just to tell the truth
but to tell the truth in love, and to tell the truth in
love means to tell it with concern not only for the
truth that is being told but with concern also for
the people it is being told to.

Frederick Buechner, *Telling the Truth*

Last month a friend of mine who took a courageous and unpopular position on a controversial subject. Unfortunately, his mailbox quickly filled with hate mail from people who didn't recognize the difference between "the truth" and their own opinion. Sadly, some of these letter bombs were signed "in Christian love."

While the letter writers had no intention to deceive my friend, were they not deceiving themselves about what it means to speak the truth in love? The apostle Paul spoke about spiritual maturity when he advised the Ephesian church, "Speaking the truth in love, *we must grow up* in every way into him who is the head, into Christ" (Ephesians 4:15 NRSV, italics mine).

Seasoning truth telling with love is a mark of maturity. That graceful form of growing up uses words to build rather than destroy. Christians are not to tear down the body of Christ with destructive prattle. I like what Frederick Buechner says about loving truthfulness: "To preach the Gospel is not just to tell the truth but to tell the truth in love, and to tell the truth in love means to tell it with concern not only for the truth that is being told but with concern also for the people it is being told to."

From personal experience, I know that it is easier to concern myself with the abstract concept of truth than with my concrete relationship to the person to whom I'm telling the truth. This is an area where my body language seems to be way beyond my conscious control.

Sometimes I can hear it in my voice on the telephone when I'm talking about something that means a great deal to me. Even if my head hasn't figured it out yet, the emotion in my voice betrays how important a particular relationship is to me. If my mouth stays moist and there is no crack in my voice when I must confront someone, then I must beware. If there is no emotion in my voice, the chances are that I would not care if that person dropped out of my life, never to be seen again. I hate it when I can't get control over those perturbations in my voice! But then lying is about control, isn't it?

Sometimes this tension spills over into my letter-writing. I caught a friend in what I believed to be (and probably was) a half-truth. What he had done so wounded me that I knew better than to answer him right away. I would not have dared to let him hear the tightly controlled rage in my voice. I couldn't have kept the tears out. Allowing my anger to cool, I wrote, edited, and reedited an E-mail message to him in return. My letter ended with the caveat that I was "speaking the truth in love." Satisfied by bedtime with both my content and my style, I double-clicked the mouse to send my missive on its way. But then I couldn't sleep.

Still angry at my friend, I kept replaying his lie in my head. When I should have been sleeping, my blood pressure was rising. I passed a miserable night.

E-mail may have simplified my life and enhanced my response time in letter writing, but I'm sorry, Bill Gates, it is no substitution for face-to-face contact. Even a voice on the telephone is better than text devoid of context. Even a cracking, emotion betraying, out-of-control voice.

Whenever my pastor has to write a difficult letter, he asks his wife to review it as a second opinion before he puts the letter in the mail. "Keep it clean," Mary tells Laurie about his choice of words. Clean not only in clarifying the truth he feels called to impart but also clean in regard to his relationship with the letter recipient.

Some of us—my pastor and I both, for example—are so passionate about the truth that we frame our choice of words more by the issue at hand than by our relationship to the recipient. Others—like the friend to whom I sent my smart bomb of an E-mail message—value relationships above issues and will first consider the effect of his words.

When we place the issue at hand above relationships and carry it to an extreme, we produce confrontation. When we place relationships above issues and carry this to an extreme, we engage in conflict avoidance. My pastor's wife exemplifies a balance between the two extremes that David Augsburger calls "carefrontation." The carefronter keeps the word path swept clean.

Truth spoken in love has the capacity to transform, for it inflects its tone with the heart, not just with the pen or keyboard. If we speak the truth with malice, our words may be received in the spirit of a lie.

I wish that the well-meaning Christians who sent that hate mail to my friend had stopped long enough to read 1 Corinthians 13. I wish I had reread it before sending my own E-mail message as well. As I have paraphrased it here for letter writers, St. Paul offers hopeful advice for loving mature truth tellers full of humility, hospitality, and discretion:

> My letter writing is patient, it is kind. My words do not uncover envy, they do not boast, they are not proud. What I write is neither rude nor self-seeking. I am not easily angered, neither do I keep old letters as records of wrongs. In taking care to frame my letters in love, I do not delight in evil but rejoice with the truth. The love of Christ that guards my words always protects those with whom I correspond, always trusts another whose heart is set on Christ, always hopes that Christ rules in their lives as well as mine, and always perseveres to find a loving way to phrase the things I need to say. (1 Corinthians 13:4–7, my adaptation)

Chapter Twenty-Two Study Questions

1. Locate a copy of a letter you sent someone when you had to tell them the truth about something they may not have wished to have faced. Rewrite that letter, and this time "keep it clean."

2. Recall an occasion when you thought you told someone the truth to deal with your anger "before the sun went down."
   a. Did you both come to peace about that situation?
   b. Would you handle that encounter differently today if you had the chance to relive it?
   c. On that occasion, were you a truth teller or merely a fact-holder?

3. What is the difference between being honest with yourself about your own feelings and telling your feelings to somebody else?

4. Is it harder to be truthful about your feelings:
    a.   with yourself?
    b.   with someone else?

5. Is it more important to be truthful about your feelings:
    a.   with yourself?
    b.   with someone else?

As a matter of fact... Well, the truth of the matter is... To tell you the truth... Let's be perfectly honest here... And that's the whole truth... It was only a little white lie... Well, the truth of the matter is... Let's be perfectly honest here... It was only a little white lie... As a matter of fact... To tell you the truth... And that's the whole truth... As a matter of fact... Well, the truth of the matter is... To tell you the truth... Let's be perfectly honest here... And that's the whole truth... It was only a little white lie... Well, the truth of the matter is... Let's be perfectly honest here... It was only a little white lie... As a matter of fact... To tell you the truth... And that's the whole truth... As a matter of fact... Well, the truth of the matter is... To tell you the truth... Let's be perfectly honest here... And that's the whole truth... It was only a little white lie... Well, the truth of the matter is...

EPILOGUE

The Anatomy Lesson

(epilogue: the anatomy lesson)

Do I go with my heart or my gut? I gotta do an
entire autopsy.

Paul Reiser, *Couplehood*

There is a fascinating painting by Rembrandt titled "The Anatomy Lesson of Dr. Tulp." On the canvas Dr. Nicholaas Tulp and his seventeenth-century entourage wear stiff, black formal attire with ruffled white collars to frame their rosy Dutch complexions. These anatomists even knew the name of their cadaver. Aris Kindt's corpse became available for his bizarre final portrait after he was hanged in Amsterdam for repeated acts of petty theft. What is most remarkable is that no one at the dissection table is looking at the cadaver.

Two of Tulp's retinue who once stared out at Rembrandt now peer out at museum visitors. Five other members of Amsterdam's senior guild of surgeons strain to see the textbook. Most interesting of all is the professor himself. Tulp's eyes stare above all their heads as if he has given this lecture a thousand times before and can recite it point by point in his deepest sleep.

Not one of those anatomy students looked at the body for his lesson. The unvarnished, ungarnished Kindt appeared too stark a subject to command their direct attention, as if he was too blatantly truthful to teach about himself. The same is true about the anatomy of our lies. We may not want to look. We may develop indirect ways to examine so stark a subject.

In this closing section, I invite you to sharpen your focus and look at our subject directly as we sum up our anatomy lesson with our heads, our hearts, and our guts. Rather than limiting ourselves to the "fitting" as a situational ethicist would, we'll examine the "right" and "good" as well:

The "right"—Scriptural principles
The "good"—Benefits that flow from applying those
    principles
The "fitting"—Where the "right" and "good" are
    leading us.

If we don't carefully examine the "right" and "good," how else can we possibly know what "fitting" might be?

Part One: A Lie Never Justified?

Our friend, H. Clay Trumbull, did not tell lies because he believed that lying was inconsistent with the character of God. That's an excellent reason to be truthful, but there also is a practical reason why God tells us not to deceive. Lying is rarely a solitary practice.

"Do not deceive *one another*" (Leviticus 19:11, NIV).

"You shall not give false testimony *against your neighbor*" (Exodus 20:16, NIV).

One person's lie can insidiously harm another, thus the appropriateness of Michael Josephson's metaphor of lies as land mines.

God commands me to tell the truth, not so that I may feel righteous before him for my obedience, but for the benefit of my neighbor. If I seek to justify myself in matters of the law, then I must stop—like the expert in the law in the parable of the Good Samaritan—and ask just who my neighbor is (Luke 10:25–37).

The benefit that my neighbor reaps from my truthfulness is not only in personal safety, but as a glimpse of the image of God: "Do not lie to each other, since you have taken off your old self with its practices and have *put on the new self, which is being renewed in knowledge in the image of its Creator*" (Colossians 3:9–10, NIV, italics mine). Thus, the commandment to love the

Lord our God with every part of our being and our neighbor as ourselves is a hymn to the restoration of the *imago Dei* in the world. Any misery I experience in prizing truth is but a birth pang in that restoration process.

Who is my neighbor when it comes to my personal truthfulness? Sometimes my neighbor is the one that I lied to or the one most immediately affected by my falsehood. But always my neighbor is the one who is most in need of a glimpse of God.

You remember Sasha, the waiter? He finally found a good-paying job. Before he left the Chowder Pot, I gave him a book that tells Crumb Bunny's story and how I became her unofficial grandma the day of her bone marrow transplantation.[1] It's a story of God's action in the world. Better late with the truth than never at all.

There were positive examples of truth's neighborliness in those opening chapters as well. Remember those women doctors who spent a weekend sharing things they had deeply hidden in their hearts? I was a good neighbor to them when I told them that story that I had always kept hidden. On Saturday night all our tears became neighborly to a young man who came to the banquet.

After dinner, a third-year medical student came to me with tears in his eyes. He wanted to tell me about a dream he had had, a promise he had made to God based on that dream, and a song he had written based on his dream and promise.

In his dream, he heard a mother weeping. He couldn't tell me about this dream without tears running down his cheeks! In response to his dream, he felt called to choose a field of medicine where he could wipe away mothers' tears. His song—that he tearfully sang for me—recalled his dream and the promise he made to God to use his skills as a doctor to dry that mother's tears.

His story touched me very deeply. What if I had held onto the glittering image of a doctor who can always control her own feelings, as if that was what was most fitting for my patients? I wouldn't have been telling the truth, would I? And yet, neither would I have intended to deceive.

If I hadn't told my story at that conference—and it wasn't easy for me to share—the sequence of events might have been quite different. That young man might have bought into the lie that big boys and big doctors don't cry. He could have filed away his dream, flushed his tears, and missed out on something special that God has in mind for him. The truth may make us miserable, but it does ultimately free us by revealing the face of God.

I'm fascinated how events of half a century ago in Europe can play such a central role in the moral life of modern pilgrims. Hitler's "Final Solution" was so unthinkable that we are still thinking about it today. In the quiet of our hearts we wonder if we would have the courage of a Bonhoeffer or a Ten Boom to defy a truly evil power.

In one study of "the righteous ones"—Gentiles who risked their own lives for the sake of Jews—a common thread was found. These neighbors were open families who had always practiced hospitality, even before the Nazi crisis. "Practice hospitality," says Paul. "Share with God's people who are in need" (Romans 12:13, NIV). Be a good neighbor with the truth.

What does my neighbor need? Sometimes my neighbor needs my words. If the prohibition against lying is for the sake of the neighbor, then is not the proclamation of truth for the same intent? The psalmist speaks of God's love and truth as protection (Psalm 40:11, NIV). But sometimes my neighbor needs my silence instead.

"Do not do anything that endangers your neighbor's life" (Leviticus 19:16, NIV). This commandment to protect stands side by side with the commandment to not bear false witness against that same neighbor.

W. H. Auden says that we are commanded to love our neighbor because "our 'natural' attitude toward the 'other' is one of either indifference or hostility."[2] Hospitality needs practice. It doesn't come to us all that naturally. Do my words offer hospitality, a neighborly hiding place?

H. Clay Trumbull had lots of neighbors in that South Carolina Confederate prison. Easily, his buddies were his neighbors, and as far as I can see, he was their hiding place. Although he made his opinion about lying clear to his friends, I see no evidence that he betrayed their escape plan to the guards.

Were Trumbull's jailers his neighbors as well? There I'm not so certain that he would agree. He spoke of their forfeiture of their social rights. The Samaritan may have been the Jew's neighbor in Jesus' eyes, but the Reb was not the Yank's neighbor in that prison camp. Some would say the same holds true today.

The neighbor that Jesus spoke of in his parable, the neighbor most in need of a glimpse of God, was the one whose life was in jeopardy. Whether or not Trumbull saw his jailer as his neighbor, he made no choices that endangered his jailer's life. By staying in jail, he did not have to lie, and he did not have to take his captor's life.

We could ask the same question for Shiprah and Puah, Rahab, and the Ten Booms, each of whom treated Jews not as despised aliens but as neighbors when their lives were in danger. But for each of these faithful women, words of mercy led to acts of civil disobedience and, in some cases, to lies.

Frankly, I think it's good to come face-to-face in these stories with the reality that the moral life isn't easy. When Jesus debated about the law with the legal experts of his time, he was offering them a reality check. In worshiping the law more than the Lawgiver, the Pharisees forgot the reason for which God gave the law. "The Sabbath was made for man, not man for the Sabbath" (Mark 2:27, NIV). The purpose of the law is to restore God's image in our "neighborhood," to make the world a safe and holy place to live.

Listen to this dream I had, for it summarizes the tensions I feel between the two commandments: not to lie, and not to endanger life. The dream happened while I was writing the section, "A Lie Never Justified?"

I was in a Middle Eastern country, visiting my friend and fellow writer Philip Yancey and his wife, Janet. Philip was on some sort of mysterious assignment there and showed me an album of photos he had taken of a restricted military installation. While the Yanceys were out, some authorities came and started to search the place. Apparently they had questioned Philip earlier and had seen a photo taken adjacent to the military installation.

I thought they suspected that Philip had been to the forbidden location. I was holding the small photo album with incriminating photos in it and wanted to get the album back into its hiding place before they saw it. If the authorities asked me about it, of course I would have to tell them the truth. After all, a lie is never justified!

As I lay on a bed, feigning sleep, trying to escape notice, an Arab woman—the landlady—rearranged the furniture back to where it had originally been before the Yanceys had moved in. She replaced a chair next to the bed where I was pretending to sleep.

I thought, "When Philip and Janet get back, we should book our airline reservations for home." But if we just booked tickets to the States without return, the authorities would be suspicious. I thought that we should book round-trip tickets, leaving before Christmas, with a return portion that we had no intention to use.

What an interesting commentary on the exceedingly complex nature of the subject. Although my behavior in the dream mimicked what Walter Kaiser suggests up to a point, I wasn't even consistent in my own dream! After I woke up, I knew in my heart that if it had been a real situation, I wouldn't be able to endanger Philip and Janet's lives. My Trumbull-like absolutism melted away when it came to my friends' survival. And, please note, that my scheme even preserved my own life from the same "evildoers."

Perhaps my faith is too small to stand with Trumbull and Nollie, but I have lived through too many other experiences where God expected me to think through from right and good to fitting. More important than all my ambivalent and conflicted actions in the dream was my wide-awake reexamination of that simple question by the light of day. *Is a lie ever justified?* Awake, I knew in my heart that I would try to be truthful without revealing what they did not directly ask for. I would not be a fact tattler. But if push came to shove, I couldn't put Philip and Janet's lives in danger.

But here is where I would depart from ethical relativists like Joseph Fletcher. *Even if I saw no alternative in that situation other than to tell a lie to save a life, I would not later claim that any lie I told was justified.* This, I think, is the same moral conclusion that Corrie ten Boom reached. Listen to what Corrie said on the subject of lying many years after her release from the concentration camp: "Can I bless a lie?" the Lord asked me in my heart. "I can only bless the truth."[3]

This was Corrie's—not Nollie's—answer from God. Not once did Corrie ten Boom seek justification for her merciful lies or even beg for a quiet conscience. "Only as I walked out of the building [after protecting the Jews] did I begin to tremble. Not because for the first time in my life I had told a conscious lie. But because it had been so dreadfully easy."[4]

The life and work of Corrie ten Boom reflected the image of God. And I hope my work and life will as well, as I seek conscientiously to be as truthful and neighborly as the law demands and holy hospitality requires.

Part Two: Truth Comes Home to Roost

An old divine named Jeremy Taylor considered it lawful to lie to children and to the mentally impaired because "they, having no powers of judging, have no right to the truth."[5] No right to the truth? I shudder when I read that.

In Scripture, "rights" are rarely assigned to those in a position of power. Job speaks of the rights of the afflicted (Job 36:6). David, Solomon, and the prophets call for the rights of the innocent, the poor, the widow, and oppressed (Psalm 82:3; Proverbs 29:7; 31:5, 8–9; Isaiah 10:2; Jeremiah 5:28). Scripture usually provides rights to the most vulnerable members of society. Those in power more often learn from the Bible what their responsibilities are.

You've heard the polarizing arguments about "childrens' rights" and "parents' rights" that are raging across the world. Those arguments speak the language of contracts. For important relationships, the Bible speaks the language of covenant.

"Contract and covenant, materially considered, appear to be first cousins," says William F. May. "Covenants cut deeper into personal identity."[6] Covenants link us to those most important "others," our most intimate neighbors. Aren't our families the ones who most need to see a glimpse of God through us?

As I listen to my friend Sherri, I hear her talking the language of marital contract. Either Art shapes up and complies with a set of negotiated standards or he ships out. If wedding vows had renewal clauses in them, as most contracts do, I can't think of a single marriage I know that would make it past the opening year. If God made contracts with the world instead of rainbow covenants, you would have to hold on to your umbrella.

God loves the truth, but he loves us too. Because God is the Truth, his covenant with us survives. He forgives. Covenants survive, truth is tellable, and truth is hearable when there is a servant relationship between the parties. That was the model that Jesus— the Way, the Truth, and the Life—chose. If husbands and wives were willing to act as spouse servers, parents were willing to be child servers, and children were willing to be parent servers from their own birth to their parents' grave, we could tell each other the truth and the world would see more of God.

Contracts look for competitors; covenants seek companions. In biblical terms, truthfulness and justice walk side by side. Both reflect the image of God. Hear it from the inspired lips of the prophet Isaiah:

> Your lips have spoken lies, and your tongue mutters wicked things. No one calls for justice; no one pleads his case with integrity. They rely on empty arguments and speak lies.... So justice is driven back, and righteousness stands at a distance; truth has stumbled in the streets, honesty cannot enter. Truth is nowhere to be found, and whoever shuns evil becomes a prey (Isaiah 59:3b,4,14–15, NIV).

When children cry, "It's not fair!" parents automatically respond with, "But life's not fair." Well, folks, perhaps our kids would listen more carefully to what we have to say about truthfulness if we showed more concern about justice.

Get out that journal you started back in chapter 1 and strike out a new page to make a graph. Next to the x-axis, write the words "loyalty and justice." Next to the y-axis, pen in the word "truthfulness." Label a diagonal line that divides the square in half "carefrontation."

If we as adults want to effect life-shaping changes in the lives of the kids we love, we must understand more about how the loyalty and justice they cherish impacts upon the words we use to frame the truth we uphold. If teens are going to grow into the likeness of Christ, they must weigh the truthful words used to express worthwhile loyalty and justice. We can pull together from our two extremes and walk a "carefrontation" line together. To stay on the line in pace together will take humility on all of our parts.

The Dude's pastor asked him to do a job, but Paulie told Bob that he had other plans that he couldn't get out of. By the time Paul got home, he was face-to-face with a collision of truthfulness and loyalty.

Paulie, who is one of the most loyal people I know, wrote in his second-year journal about lying, "It got to me. So I called

[Pastor Bob] up at home and told him I [had] changed my plans. But I did lie to him twice. This is no big deal thing he asked [me to do] and I will enjoy doing it, but I'm still [annoyed] at why I lied [to him]. That bugged me."

I don't think that the Dude would have even kept a journal if I hadn't been honest with him and the other kids about my own struggle to always be truthful. It helps kids to have adults in their lives who admit that they're not perfect.

Time is a gracious gift that waters the seed of truth that has been planted and is germinating. Hear the wisdom of the Dude as he admits that he was wrong in seeking justification for a lie: "All I wanted was to be kind of right and my friends made me feel that way. I was wrong in wanting to be right."

For servants of truth and servants of each other, there is always room for a covenant.

Part Three: It's an Ethical Jungle Out There

Remember our old friend Acid Warlock, the armchair ethical nihilist? "Today's world wouldn't work with morals," the fellow said. And Larry, the man with two ethical hats who has come to believe that "integrity and honesty don't work at work"? As broad a discipline as ethics may be, both of them identify one virtue—truthfulness—as the stumbling block to jungle-style ethics.

Have you ever looked the word *ethics* up in the dictionary?

- decency
- moral principles
- moral practice
- code of right and wrong
- social values
- social laws
- mores
- conduct
- morality

And the adjective *ethically*?

- decently
- honorably
- morally
- justly
- properly
- scrupulously
- righteously
- conscientiously
- appropriately

Like "truthfulness," none of these are currently popular words.

Without a doubt, the most unpopular people I spoke with this year are the truth tellers. One doctor who is scrupulous about communications with his patients referred to himself as a "pathological truth teller." Now, I know that he didn't mean that he got a sadistic thrill out of telling people things that they really don't want to hear. But his choice of words hints at how extra-from-ordinary his colleagues and patients consider his honest approach.

Look back at the examples of lies in "It's an Ethical Jungle Out There." Whether or not the prevaricators considered their departures from the truth "lies of necessity," they surely weren't "beneficent lies." They were lies to get ahead of the next guy.

The greatest irony of all is the little known fact that good ethics help business. Perhaps Greg's MBA professors should be telling their students that, instead of nudging them into fudgery. Recent changes in the federal sentencing guidelines for white-collar crime clearly signal that the public has a low tolerance for unethical market conduct. Neither do customers return to a car dealership that has lied to them before. Citing positive examples of commercial success linked to high ethical business standards, corporate ethics consultant Larry Ponemon claims that, "People do not want to buy from, work for, or invest in companies believed to be unethical."[7]

It pays to see your clients as your neighbors and reflect the image of God in your dealings with them. In the interest of good business, it's time for a little downsizing of corporate duplicity. If the academic ethicists have failed us by falling for fuzz, we need to become boardroom and kitchen ethicists ourselves. Decency begins with you and me.

"The truth," says Lee Strobel, "is that the ethical temperature of a company, an industry, or an entire nation will notch up only when individuals make the commitment, one by one, to morality in business"[8]—the "trickle-up effect" I proposed to you in the prologue. If Strobel—who was for many years the legal journalist with the *Chicago Tribune*—can say that about the corporate world he knows, how can your world and mine be less possible to transform?

Stephen Carter, a colleague at Yale and nationally lauded constitutional law scholar, is a classroom ethicist. Carter is not afraid to speak out about personal integrity. Integrity, says Carter is "discern[ing] what is right and what is wrong; ... acting on what you have discerned, even at personal cost; and ... saying openly that you are acting on your understanding of right."[9]

Discern. Act. Share. I agree. The man is talking about telling the truth.

There may be a personal price to pay in downsizing duplicity, but we can't afford not to pay it. What's more, it is the honest thing to do.

Part Four: The Truth Always Warranted?

What if I got my ethical act together and determined to always tell the truth? What if, as well, my truthful words were always spoken carefully and in love? Would anyone be listening to what I have to say?

The prisoner before Pilate answers that if you would listen to him, you would hear the truth. He, Jesus, testifies to the truth, and everyone who is on the side of truth will listen to what he has to say.

But Pilate wasn't listening to Jesus the day that Jesus went on trial. There's a problem when you listen to this fellow Jesus. When he speaks, Jesus "says something that leaves us muttering, 'That's outrageous.'"[10]

"Outrageous" is the opposite of "ringing true."

Perhaps if we understood how we judge truthfulness in others, we would understand why we sometimes raise an eyebrow to Jesus when he says to us, "I tell you the truth," as if what Jesus says is not warranted.

In her novel *Absolute Truths*, Susan Howatch invites us to consider how we evaluate the truthfulness of others.[11] Two of her characters skirt the margins of the law as they attempt to protect the reputation of a troubled cleric. Before the police have a chance to search the home of a brutally beaten pastor, his bishop removed items that may or may not have been relevant to the assault. Chances are that they were. To be certain, there would have been a scandal if the media got wind of the locked box of pornographic materials the bishop found hidden in the pastor's bedroom.

As the bishop rationalizes withholding this erotic cache from the authorities, he tests theories in his mind that he might present to the police. Finally, he finds a plausible story and says to himself, "This assessment had the ring of truth. I finally began to relax."

Let's look at the reasons why that fictional bishop—or we—might find that a particular statement "rings true":

- True-sounding statements sound logical.
- True-sounding statements fit with our own worldview.
- True-sounding statements make us feel comfortable and reduce our wariness.

But the bishop's true-sounding statement was patently misleading and intentionally so. Lulled by the bishop's reputation,

listening to his half-true recitation, the police did not learn important facts surrounding the assault.

Let us move from that fictional English vicarage back to
Gabbatha's historic judgment hall. In a world of many truths and
half-truths, Frederick Buechner says that Pilate is hungry for
truth itself. Or failing that, "At least that there is no truth."[12] But
Pilate wasn't hungry enough.

You and I, friend reader, can play an important role in this
cosmic drama. Join me as a jury member for the most important
trial in all of human history. It's time for us to take our seats in
the jury box as the trial of Jesus Christ begins. The prosecutor is
about to make his opening statement. . . .

"Ladies and gentlemen of the jury, the prosecution is most
willing to allow the prisoner, Jesus (the so-called Christ), to
speak for himself. We need not wade through all his copious
prior testimony. Focus instead on those statements where the
defendant prefaces his remarks with the words (depending on
your preferred Bible translation; it makes no difference!):

- 'Verily I say unto thee' (KJV), or
- 'Truly I tell you' (NRSV), or
- 'I tell you solemnly' (JERUSALEM), or
- 'Believe me' (PHILLIPS), or most simply
- 'I tell you the truth' (NIV).

"You are the finders of fact in this case. People, you tell me
if this is an honest man speaking. Determine for yourself if Jesus'
statements are: (1) logical; (2) fit your personal experience; or
(3) put your mind at ease.

"First, ladies and gentlemen of the jury, let us examine Jesus'
statements for simple logic. Listen as I read his own 'less-is-more'
concepts as recorded by Matthew, Mark, Luke, and John (whom
his own defense counsel has stipulated to be reliable witnesses):

- 'This poor widow has put more into the treasury than all
  the others' (Mark 12:43 NIV; Luke 21:3).

- 'Among those born of women there has not risen anyone greater than John the Baptist; yet he who is least in the kingdom of heaven is greater than he' (Matthew 11:11 NIV).
- 'Only those who change and become like children will enter the kingdom of heaven' (Matthew 18:3; John 3:3).
- 'It is hard for the wealthy to enter the kingdom of heaven' (Matthew 19:23).
- 'If you have faith as small as a mustard seed, you can say to this mountain, "Move from here to there" and it will move. Nothing will be impossible for you' (Matthew 17:20 NIV; 21:21; Mark 11:23).

"I ask you, members of the jury, where is the logic in those statements? No wonder Jesus had to preface his words with a claim that he was being truthful! This 'verily, verily' stuff is the same as if I were to say to you, 'I kid you not.'[13] Just who does Jesus think he's kidding? Not intelligent men and women like yourselves! Logic alone tells us that less is less and more is more.

"Next, my fellow citizens, Jesus says that outsiders are insiders. How does that fit with your own experience, your community's view of the world? Listen to this fellow's own outrageous words:

- 'Sometimes those outside the fold of the faithful express more faithfulness than those within' (Matthew 8:10).
- 'The sheep owner is happier about that one sheep that had wandered away [and returned] than about the ninety-nine that didn't wander' (Matthew 18:13).
- 'The tax collectors and the prostitutes will enter the kingdom of God ahead of religious leaders' (Matthew 21:31).
- 'As a memorial to her, wherever this gospel is preached throughout the world, the story will be told of the woman who poured out expensive perfume on Jesus head' (Matthew 26:13; Mark 14:9).

"Do you hear how he insults you, my fellow citizens? He would rather dine with the scum of this city than people like yourselves. That last story is a prime example. Why, his own longtime associate, the honorable Judas Iscariot, was appalled by the waste of expensive perfume that could have been sold to feed the poor. Here he was, dining with Jesus at the home of our esteemed friend and Pharisee Simon, when this woman broke into their dinner party. Outrageous, I tell you! So outrageous that Mr. Iscariot felt compelled to come to us and turn state's evidence against his teacher.

"The prosecution will not insult you by offering tax collectors and prostitutes as witnesses to support the state's case. We would not affront you by asking you to believe their testimony. No, ladies and gentlemen, the prosecution will offer you instead religious leaders, expert witnesses in the law, upstanding members of the community—honorable people like yourselves.

"Thirdly, people, ask yourselves whether these statements made by the defendant put your minds at ease:

- 'Not one stone [of the temple buildings] will be left on another; every one will be thrown down' (Matthew 24:2 NIV).
- 'One of you will betray me' (Matthew 26:21 NIV; Mark 14:18; John 13:21).
- 'We testify to what we have seen, but still you people do not accept our testimony' (John 3:11 NIV).
- 'Why does this generation ask for a miraculous sign?... [N]o sign will be given to it' (Mark 8:12 NIV).
- Those who make a point of doing their good deeds in public receive their full reward then and there (Matthew 6:2, 5, 16).
- Lack of hospitality for Jesus' followers who preach his Gospel of the kingdom will be judged more harshly than Sodom and Gomorrah (Matthew 10:15).
- 'Unless you eat the flesh of the Son of Man and drink his blood, you have no life in you' (John 6:53 NIV).

- 'Watch out for the teachers of the law' (Mark 12:38 NIV).
- 'All this [judgment] will come upon this generation [of snakes and vipers]' (Matthew 23:36 NIV).
- 'I don't know you [foolish virgins]' (Matthew 25:12 NIV).

"Ladies and gentlemen, Jesus has called you 'snakes and vipers'! You, upstanding members of our community, he calls 'foolish virgins'! This outcast Galilean would cast you out of the heavenly kingdom!

"Members of the jury, I plan to call no other witnesses. Listen to Jesus' own words. Use your own experience. When in your deliberations the time for judgment finally comes, answer this one simple question and you will have your verdict: Does what this man Jesus says ring true in your ears?

"On his own words and your judgment I rest my entire case."

If we judged Jesus' words by our culture's standards for truthfulness, a modern jury would not set him free. But Jesus is not concerned with satisfying culture's demands. Neither should you be. He came to set culture's prisoners free. That sort of truth is always warranted. How verily outrageous.

Part Five: The Language of the Lie

"Let words work the earth of my heart," says poet Kathleen Norris.[14]

Words not only work my heart, they also work the heart of God.

"In the beginning was the WORD and the WORD was with God, and the WORD was God. . . . By God's WORD the heavens existed and the earth was formed out of water and by water. . . . The WORD of the Lord stands forever. . . . He has revealed his WORD to Jacob, his laws and decrees to Israel. . . . The WORD of God is living and active, sharper than any double-edged sword, it penetrates even to dividing soul and spirit, joints and marrow; it judges the thoughts and attitudes of the heart. . . . He is dressed in a robe dipped in blood, and his name is the WORD of God."

Words are far too important to hand them over to a lie, no matter how fitting the situation may seem at the time. I can't move my words around as I alone see fit, like pawns on a cosmic chessboard. Words are a gift for which we must accept accountability if they are to reveal the image of God.

The way we express our ideas distinguishes us from the lower animals. When Babu uses his expressive face or his counter-tenor monosyllabic obligato to communicate with me, he makes his thoughts perfectly clear. He doesn't play games. And Babu doesn't lie. Language games belong to those of us gifted with higher reason.

Have you ever kept a private diary? I did many years ago, and I can't say that I was totally honest in those volumes that were for my eyes only. Neither was I totally honest when I shared my story aloud with friends.

Before I presented my story for human consumption, I would edit it, hone my yarns, spit on them, and polish them each time I talked about the "real me." I shaped my life's story to the way I wanted to hear it—and to be heard. Autobiography, after all, is the most unfaithful form of literature.

Ironically, it was while working in the hospital that I first saw that there is a striking similarity between what I read in the Bible—God's diary—and the lives of my patients. In the Bible and on a cancer ward, I saw stories unfold with all the blemishes exposed. In neither place was there cosmetic surgery for the soul. The people in Scripture and the patients on my ward were naked, vulnerable folks. Not like you and me—the healthy, the intelligent, who clothe ourselves in words to conceal who we really are.

This has been a very different type of journal. From the first entry I knew that it was not for-my-eyes-only. I've seen how ugly some of my words are, how hastily I speak them, and how I need to be accountable for the things that I say. Not every word I use displays the image of God. Not even when I tell the truth.

Although my editor didn't know it at the time I began, he was part of my plan to be accountable to you and to God. It takes a lot of trust to share raw, unedited text in which I sometimes prattled wildly en route to my next useful point. But I didn't want to clean up my journal before Lyn saw it. I wanted to be honest to God and honest with you.

Oh, the birth pangs that bring the image of God into the world through an act of hospitality for my neighbor! "He chose to give us birth through the WORD of truth." Let words continue to work the earth of my heart in everything I say and write and hear. There are too many words in this world that "I'm sorry" just can't erase.

Part Six: Honest Hearts

"What's a 'poser'?" a confused young teen asked one of her friends. All the kids she knew were using the term. A "poser" is what you and I used to call a phony.

Posers can't decide what they want to be so they pretty much pretend to be something they aren't. He may dress like a surfer, but never have ridden a wave. She may look like a preppy, but never have cracked a book. A poser is about the worst thing a kid can call someone today, including each other, including themselves. "Who cares who you are," wrote one of my teen buddies in her journal, "as long as you are you?"

The apostle Paul tells us to put away our posing:

> You were taught, with regard to your former way of life, to put off your old self, which is being corrupted by its deceitful desires; to be made new in the attitude of your minds; and to put on the new self, created to be like God in true righteousness and holiness. *Therefore each of you must put off falsehood and speak truthfully to his neighbor*, for

we are all members of one body (Ephesians 4:22–25 NIV, italics mine).

In the successful moral life, truthfulness and neighborliness always seem to run hand in hand. "How would you define success?" one of Susan Howatch's characters asks in her novel *Glittering Images*.

> "Success is pursuing one's calling to the best of one's ability."
>
> "Which self?"
>
> "One's true self. . . . One dedicates one's true self to serving God and one strives to do His will."
>
> "How would your true self define failure?"
>
> "Locking up one's true self in order to live a lie."[15]

I confess: Other than the natural flow of a book, there's a reason why the section on honest hearts comes at the end. Writing and thinking about my feelings are not my strong points.

"When you tell stories about other people," Philip Yancey once wrote to me, "a simple eloquence rises up to carry the story. The closer I get to Diane Komp and her feelings and true thoughts, the more a smokescreen of words goes up."

Philip is a faithful neighbor to me, telling me a truth I do not particularly want to hear. I watched that smokescreen go up in my journal, even with my editor looking on. It's easier to be honest in my head than my heart. This will be a lifelong struggle for me, not an instant "aha" conversion-type experience, to become totally honest about the real me.

When I am dying, like John Powell, "I want to remember the times when I was real and honest, when I shared myself in an open self-disclosure as an act of love."[16] Hold me accountable, friend reader. Be my faithful neighbor. If you ever find a smokescreen in my words getting in your way of seeing the real me, let me know.

And when I die, let me be me. Don't dress me up in a smart, dark FBI suit or powder my cheeks an incorruptible shade of salmon bisque.[17] That wouldn't be neighborly. Don't spoil my final chance to declare who I really am. You'll find my black-and-white-and-rabbit patchwork sweater in my bedroom dresser, third drawer from the top on the right.

When both my lips and pen are silent, let me tell the truth about who I was and who I am and who I yet will be. Let me reflect the image of God—approachable, touchable—for everyone to see.

(endnotes)

Prologue: Anatomy of a Lie

1. Sandra Wilson, *Released from Shame* (Downers Grove, Ill.: Inter-Varsity, 1990), 83.

Chapter 1: When Johnny Didn't Come Marching Home Again

1. Charles Frazier, *Cold Mountain* (New York: Atlantic Monthly, 1997), 105.
2. H. Clay Trumbull, *A Lie Never Justifiable: A Study in Ethics* (Philadelphia: John D. Wattles, 1893), 2.
3. Trumbull, *A Lie Never Justifiable*, 5.
4. Trumbull, *A Lie Never Justifiable*, 6.

Chapter 2: The Hebrews' Midwives and a Canaanite Whore

1. Trumbull, *A Lie Never Justifiable*, 36.
2. Robert Jay Lipton, *The Nazi Doctors: Medical Killing and the Psychology of Genocide* (New York: Basic Books, 1986), 52, 54.
3. Dietrich Bonhoeffer, *Ethics* (New York: Macmillan, 1955), 64–65, 366.
4. Trumbull, *A Lie Never Justifiable*, 38.

Chapter 3: The Saints of the Béjé

1. Corrie ten Boom with John and Elizabeth Sherrill, *The Hiding Place* (Old Tappen, N.J.: Fleming H. Revell, 1971).
2. Ten Boom, *The Hiding Place*, 66.
2. Ten Boom, *The Hiding Place*, 111.
4. Walter C. Kaiser Jr., Peter H. Davids, F. F. Bruce, and Manfred T. Brauch, *Hard Sayings of the Bible* (Downers Grove, Ill.: InterVarsity, 1996), 210.
5. Ten Boom, *The Hiding Place*, 90–91.
6. Ten Boom, *The Hiding Place*, 111–112.
7. Ten Boom, *The Hiding Place*, 129.
8. Ten Boom, *The Hiding Place*, 29.

9. Visitors are welcome at the Béjé today. For further information about the Ten Boom Museum, contact Stichting Corrie ten Boomhuis, P. O. Box 2237, 2002 CE Haarlem, Holland.

Chapter 4: A Dining Room Brocade

1. Cathy Schrull, "A Fine Old Family Tradition," from the musical *Never Alone*. Reprinted by permission of the author.

2. Joseph Fletcher, *Situation Ethics* (Philadelphia: Westminster, 1966), 28, 147.

3. Michael Josephson, quoted in Fred Brunning, "The Truth, The Whole Truth and Nothing But the Truth," *Newsday,* (April 21, 1997), B06.

Chapter 5: Doktor Di Meets Bad Dude Paul

1. Josh McDowell and Bob Hostetler, *Right from Wrong: What You Need to Know to Help Youth Make Right Choices* (Dallas: Word, 1994), 6.

Chapter 6: Mixed Signals

1. Jason Gaes, *My Book for Kids With Cansur* (Melius & Peterson, 1989).

Chapter 7: Holy Deadlock

1. Stanley Hauerwas and William Willimon, *Where Resident Aliens Live: Exercises for Christian Practice* (Nashville: Abington, 1996), 85–86.

2. The concept of "spouse-serving" is introduced by Dave Goetz in "Heart & Soul: Truth and Consequences: My Wife's Honesty Was the Slap in the Face I Didn't Want—but Needed," *Marriage Partnership* (winter 1996, vol. 13, no. 4), 12.

Chapter 8: Family Secrets

1. Sandra D. Wilson, *Released from Shame* (Downers Grove, Ill.: InterVarsity, 1990), 189.

Chapter 9: Eloping Home

1. Erik Erikson, "Identity and the Life Cycle," *Psychological Issues* (1:1,1959), 74–76.

Chapter 10: The Nudge Fudge

1. William V. Hayes, quoted in "Navy Midshipman Punished for Cheating, Not for Telling the Truth," *The Palm Beach Post* (May 16, 1994), 9A.

2. George Barna, *The Barna Report: What Americans Believe* (Ventura: Regal, 1991), 83–85.

3. Gene Edward Veith, *Postmodern Times: A Christian Guide to Contemporary Culture* (Wheaton, Ill.: Crossways, 1994), 51.

4. *United Press International* (November 2, 1981), Dateline: Washington.

5. Veith, *Postmodern Times,* 58.

6. *USA Today* (October 1996).

7. Melissa Jakubowski, quoted in "Honesty Not Always the Best Policy; Finals Week Puts Teachers in Bind," *Daily Egyptian* (December 7, 1975).

8. *Yale Bulletin & Calendar* (September 8–15, 1997), 6.

9. John Crewdson, "Disclosures of Fraud Rock Gene Project," *Chicago Tribune* (October 29, 1996).

Chapter 11: Business As Unusual

1. Peta Penson, "Lying: A Fact of Life in Today's Workplace," *Jacksonville Business Journal* (March 10, 1997).

2. See chapter on deception in Don Rabon, *Interviewing and Interrogation* (Durham: Carolina Academic Press, 1992), 131.

3. David Kocieniewski, quoted in "Perjury Dividend: New York Pays the Price," *New York Times* (January 5, 1997), 1.

Chapter 12: Duplicitous Divines

1. Nathaniel Hawthorne, *The Scarlet Letter* (New York: Penguin, 1986), 62.

2. Dietrich Bonhoeffer, *Ethics* (New York: Macmillan, 1955), 366.

3. Trumbull, *A Lie Never Justifiable,* 213.

Chapter 13: A Lawyer with His Torts on Fire

1. Carmine DeSena, *Lies: The Whole Truth* (New York: Putnam, 1993), 115.

2. James Patterson and Peter Kim, *The Day America Told the Truth*, 142–3.

Chapter 14: Busybodies and Other Fact Tattlers

1. Robert Coles, *The Moral Intelligence of Children: How to Raise a Moral Child* (New York: Random House, 1997), 7.
2. Annie Ortlund, *Children Are Wet Cement* (Grand Rapids: Spire, 1981).

Chapter 15: Varnish and Garnish

1. David Nyberg, *The Varnished Truth: Truth Telling and Deceiving in Ordinary Life* (Chicago: University of Chicago Press, 1993), 10.
2. Henry Cloud, *Changes That Heal* (Grand Rapids: Zondervan 1990), 23.
3. Karl Kraus, *Sprüche und Widersprüche,* ch. 9 (1909); tr. in *Half-Truths and One-And-A-Half-Truths,* "Lord, Forgive Them . . . ," ed. by Harry Zohn, (1976).
4. Meg Greenfield, "Getting High on Secrecy," *Newsweek* (February 23, 1987), 82.
5. *NPR Morning Edition* (June 17, 1997).

Chapter 16: No-Fault Syntax

1. John Leo, "Watch Out For That Language: He Who Controls the Terminology Controls the Outcome," *Charleston Daily Mail* (February 11, 1997), 4A.
2. Paul Van der Maas and Gerrit van dern Wal, "Euthanasia and Physician-Assisted Suicide in the Netherlands," *New England Journal of Medicine* (336:1386–1387, 1997).
3. Hannah More, *Religion of the Heart* (New Orleans: Paraclete, 1996), 129.

Chapter 17: Jihad Journalism

1. Norman Mailer, quoted in Carmine DeSena, *Lies: The Whole Truth* (New York: Putnam, 1993), 81.

Chapter 18: From Borrowed Feathers to Stolen Words

1. Helen Keller, quoted in Joseph P. Lash, *Helen and Teacher: The Story of Helen Keller and Annie Sullivan Macy* (New York: Addison-Wesley, 1997).
2. Helen Keller, quoted in Jim Swan, "Touching Words: Helen Keller, Plagiarism, Authorship," *The Construction of Authorship:*

Textual Appropriation in Law and Literature, eds: Martha Woodmansee and Peter Jaszi, (Durham, N.C.: Duke University Press, 1994), 65.

3. Thomas Mallon, *Stolen Words: Forays into the Origins and Ravages of Plagiarism* (New York: Tickner & Fields, 1989), xi.

4. John Leo, "This Column is Mostly True," *US News & World Report* (December 16, 1996), 17.

Chapter 19: Dented Discipline

1. "Sayings of the Desert Fathers," quoted in Kathleen Norris, *Cloister Walk* (New York: Riverhead Books, 1996), 135.

2. Norris, *Cloister Walk,* 126.

3. Norris, *Cloister Walk,* 136.

Chapter 20: Read My Lips

1. Korey's painting is on the cover of Diane Komp, *A Window to Heaven: When Children See Life in Death* (Grand Rapids: Zondervan, 1992).

2. William Gates, *The Road Ahead* (New York: Viking Press, 1995).

3. Douglas Groothuis, "It Takes More Than a Virtual Village: Why Neo-Nazis Love the Internet," *Books and Culture* (May/June, vol. 3, no. 3), 14. See also Groothuis's longer treatment of the subject in *The Soul in Cyberspace* (Grand Rapids: Baker Books, 1996).

4. See Don Rabon, *Interviewing and Interrogation* (Durham: Carolina Academic Press, 1992), 138.

5. Rabon, *Interviewing and Interrogation,* 133.

6. Rabon, *Interviewing and Interrogation,* 25.

7. Mark H. McCormack, *What They Don't Teach You at Harvard Business School* (New York: Random House, 1985).

Chapter 21: Hearing the Truth with Courage

1. Nyberg, *The Varnished Truth,* 18.

2. Nyberg, *The Varnished Truth,* 84.

Epilogue: The Anatomy Lesson

1. Diane Komp, *Images of Grace* (Grand Rapids: Zondervan, 1993). Six years after her successful bone marrow transplantation, Crumb Bunny is a happy and healthy schoolgirl.

2. W. H. Auden, *A Certain World* (New York: Viking, 19–70) (out of print).

3. Corrie ten Boom, *Tramp for the Lord* (Old Tappen: Fleming Revell, 1986), 107.

4. Ten Boom, *The Hiding Place,* 66.

5. Jeremy Taylor, "Ducor Dubitantium," in *Works, X.*, 103, cited in Trumbull, *A Lie Never Justifiable,* 115.

6. William F. May, *The Physician's Covenant* (Philadelphia: Westminster, 1983), 119.

7. Larry Ponemon, quoted in Interview in *Integrity,* newsletter of the KPMG Business Ethics Institute (Three Chestnut Ridge Road, Montvale, NJ 07645).

8. Lee Strobel, *God's Outrageous Claims* (Grand Rapids: Zondervan 1997), 51.

9. Stephen Carter, *Integrity* (New York: Basic Books, 1996), 7.

10. Strobel, *God's Outrageous Claims,* 7.

11. Susan Howatch, *Absolute Truths* (New York: Ballantine, 1994), 71.

12. Frederick Buechner, *Telling the Truth: The Gospel as Tragedy, Comedy, and Fairy Tale* (San Francisco: HarperCollins, 1977), 14.

13. In his chapter "The Process of Deception" in *Interviewing and Interrogation,* 143, law enforcement instructor Don Rabon lists "excessive assertions of truthfulness" as indicators of deception for which the investigator should listen.

14. Kathleen Norris, *Cloister Walk,* (New York: Riverhead Books, 1996), 144–145.

15. Susan Howatch, *Glittering Images* (New York: Ballantine, 1987), 47.

16. John Powell, *Will the Real Me Please Stand Up* (Chicago: Thomas More, 1985), 214.

17. For other incorruptible shades used by the funeral industry, read Evelyn Waugh's humorous novel *The Loved One: An Anglo-American Tragedy* (Boston: Little Brown, 1948).

Breakfast for the Heart
*Meditations to Nourish
Your Soul*

Diane M. Komp, M.D.

This is a book of meditations with
space provided for you to keep a
journal of your own spiritual
growth.

Hardcover 0-310-20916-1

A Window to Heaven
When Children See Life in Death
Diane M. Komp, M.D.

This is a first-person account of how a
pediatrician found God through the
lives of her patients.

Hardcover 0-310-58970-3

Images of Grace
*A Pediatrician's Trilogy of Faith,
Hope, and Love*

Diane M. Komp, M.D.

This complete collection of Dr.
Komp's three popular books, now in
one volume, is about a physician's
experience of faith with seriously ill
children and their families.

Softcover 0-310-20699-5

ZondervanPublishingHouse
Grand Rapids, Michigan
http://www.zondervan.com

A Division of HarperCollins*Publishers*

We want to hear from you. Please send your comments about this
book to us in care of the address below. Thank you.

ZondervanPublishingHouse
Grand Rapids, Michigan 49530
http://www.zondervan.com